Greta

Greta

Selena Fragassi

EPIC INK

Previous: Greta at the Met Gala, May 2024.

Greta walking on the red carpet of the 70th Annual Cannes Film Festival in France, May 2017.

Contents

INTRODUCTION: The 1.45 Billion Dollar Question   7

TAKE 1: A Star Is Born   23

TAKE 2: Behind the Scenes   47

TAKE 3: In Front of the Camera   75

TAKE 4: The Holy Film Trifecta   113

TAKE 5: The Future Is Waiting   181

Filmography   191

Awards and Nominations   194

Sources   197

Photo Credits   202

Acknowledgments   205

About the Author   207

Introduction

The 1.45 Billion Dollar Question

"Literally the worst thing that can happen is it's terrible and nobody likes it and it bankrupts the studio . . . but [is that] as bad as not making it? Maybe not."

—Greta speaking with *60 Minutes* about the risks of making *Barbie*

On January 23, 2024, *Barbie* fans, Greta Gerwig devotees, movie critics, and feminists everywhere were ready to burn it all down—including the Dreamhouse—when the acclaimed director of the hugely successful blockbuster was excluded from the Best Director category during nominations for the 96th Annual Academy Awards. Loaded words like "snubbed" and "robbed" drowned the internet in the days and weeks after, with the Associated Press even declaring the blatant omission "one of the biggest shocks in recent memory."

Forget for a minute that the accomplished director was already heralded for her work, previously nominated in the same divisive category for 2017's *Lady Bird*, and likewise snubbed for her acclaimed 2019 adaptation of Louisa May Alcott's *Little Women*. Forget that both of those earlier titles were more or less indie films and *Barbie* was her massive breakthrough into the mainstream, delivering the highest-grossing film of all-time for one major studio empire, Warner Bros. Forget even that *Barbie* brought in a total worldwide gross revenue of $1.45 billion and was ushered into the short list of the fifty-five films that have crossed the $1 billion threshold (currently listed at #15, just after the *Avengers* franchise, *Titanic*, and *Avatar*).

Greta attending the European premiere of *Barbie* in London, England, July 2023.

Maybe if we lived in the parallel universe of *Barbie*, Greta's name would've been included in the best director category. In Barbieland, women are powerful decision-makers and Dreamhouse homeowners, and everything is a happy pink paradise. In *Barbie*'s world, there is also room for more than one woman at the top—a counterpoint to real life, in which some hypothesized that *Anatomy of a Fall* director Justine Triet perhaps "filled the quota" for nominated female directors at the 2024 Oscars, being offered the "one and only" director nod allotted for women.

In fact, in the ninety-six-year history of the Academy, there has been only one year in which two women were nominated at the same time: 2021, when both Chloé Zhao (*Nomadland*) and Emerald Fennell (*Promising Young Woman*) were included on the short list. Chloé ended up winning the director category that year, while *Nomadland* also received the Best Picture award. That stark fact is only usurped by the fact that, in the ninety-six-year history of the Academy, only eight women directors *total* have been nominated, with Jane Campion being the sole recipient of two nominations in that group, for 1993's *The Piano* and 2021's *The Power of the Dog*. When Jane took home the award in 2022, it also marked the one and only time that women directors won in back-to-back years.

"It's no secret that the Academy Awards has often functioned like a (white) boys' club for American motion pictures," said *PureWow* in a rundown of the highly inequitable female director history. Greta, for all intents and purposes, was just one of the newest tangled fibers in that complicated web.

Within the maelstrom of *Barbie*'s supposed "backlash" and "controversy" was also the fact that Barbie herself, Margot Robbie, was ignored for a Best Actress nomination—even more insulting since she was the singular Hollywood figurehead who spearheaded the project ever since securing the rights from Mattel in 2018.

Of course, there was another point of view regarding *Barbie*, which even Greta herself echoed: The film *was* handsomely nominated, eight times over, in a range of categories, including the crème de la crème, Best Picture.

GRETA

Is Ken Next?

Although the core of *Barbie* was to create a story for the famous leading lady, Greta and her writing partner/husband Noah Baumbach were adamant about their love for Ken. "I love Ken, we love Ken. We also take Ken's position quite seriously," Greta said during her *60 Minutes* segment. The two were so tuned-in to the character they created that they also had a singular vision for who could play him, writing Ryan Gosling's name over and over in the margin of their script as a sort of casting vision board.

Just as they put their all into writing Barbie into a three-dimensional character, they did the same for Ken. "We had way too much material," Greta admitted to *60 Minutes*. So, could a movie on the blonde, tan, toned heartthrob be next? "Don't give it away because we might . . ." Noah said in the interview, before cutting himself off and leaving the suspense hanging. When reporter Sharyn Alfonsi pressed the couple on the possibility of a full Ken movie, they skirted around it, saying they "can't comment," with Greta adding, "I guess we'll see."

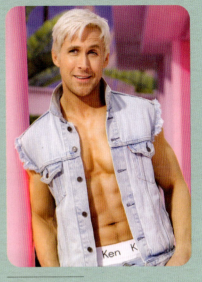

Ryan Gosling as Ken in *Barbie*.

There were also *Barbie* noms for Best Costume Design, Production Design, and two for Best Original Song, as well as nods for supporting actor Ryan Gosling and supporting actress America Ferrera. Greta and her husband/writing partner Noah Baumbach were also nominated in the Best Adapted Screenplay category. As the film's producer, Margot Robbie was part of the Oscar-nominated team for Best Picture. But, in the end, the movie only walked away with one honor: Best Original Song for the Billie Eilish and Finneas O'Connell–penned "What Was I Made For?"

INTRODUCTION

But that just made Greta's snub all the more confusing. How could a movie be up for Best Picture without the very person who'd helmed it being recognized? To quote Billy Crystal, who stood up for Barbra Streisand upon her similar snub in 1992, "Did this film direct itself?"

As Jimmy Kimmel all but reiterated as host of the 2024 Oscars telecast some thirty-plus years later, "Now, Barbie is a feminist icon thanks to Greta Gerwig, who many believe should have been nominated for best director," he shared, then scolded the audience when they began applauding. "I know you're clapping, but you're the ones who didn't vote for her, by the way. Don't act like you had nothing to do with it." According to the *New York Times*, part of the issue was the makeup of the exclusive peer voting board itself. As the periodical noted, "the snub was delivered by the directors branch, which is made up of just 587 voters, about a quarter of which are women."

Ryan Gosling—one of the loudest members of Greta's supportive choir—astutely posted on X (formerly Twitter) after the Academy Award nominations were released, "There is no Barbie movie without Greta Gerwig and Margot Robbie, the two people most responsible for this history-making, globally-celebrated film . . . To say that I'm disappointed that they are not nominated in their respective categories would be an understatement."

The simple truth is that to make a movie about such an iconic yet polarizing doll could have gone so many different—and possibly disastrous—ways: an animated romp, pandering to the Pixar audience; an about-face caped crusader narrative, pandering to the Marvel audience; a forced biopic, pandering to the art-house audience; a poorly executed rom-com that had the same sad *Melrose Place* saga so many of us have

> "[*Barbie*] is meant to be a big-hearted thing, even though it's poking fun at everyone."

Ryan Gosling, Margot Robbie, and Greta on the set of *Barbie*, June 2022.

already given Barbie on our own as children. Maybe even a fact-based documentary which could've been interesting, but as flat as the doll itself.

What Greta gave us was a nuanced, character-driven, contemporary girl-power tour de force full of heart, humor, and the kind of wit only a well-read bibliophile like Greta could deliver. In an interview with *60 Minutes* in 2023, she even referenced a Greek comedy as her defense for the *Barbie* screenplay and some of the "anti-men" criticism. "The movie is meant to be a big-hearted thing, even though it's poking fun at everyone. This is not man-hating any more than Aristophanes' *Lysistrata* was man-hating. Which does not sound like a sick burn when you say it out loud like that," she said during the interview, laughing at her own geek moment.

What Greta gave us with *Barbie* was a universal story that appealed to Boomers and Alphas alike, allowing all audience members to finally

INTRODUCTION | 11

see dimension in the plastic doll whose clean slate children have been asked to fill in over the decades. While Ruth Handler and Mattel may have birthed Barbie in 1959, Greta finally gave her life.

Through her penchant for careful, 360-degree storytelling and a focus on character development, Greta proverbially took Barbie out of her box and transformed her from a toy into the human and the "complex icon" the director believed her to be. As such, *Barbie* was not only entertaining, but also rich with existential pondering. In a review that again pointed to the literary references so deep in Greta's psyche, *W* magazine hailed the movie as a "Shakespearean Barbieland." Who would've thought the doll could be so deep?

"The vision for Barbie obviously started sixty-four years ago, but Greta bringing it into the world today in the way that only Greta Gerwig can is what makes this movie worth making right now," Margot Robbie told

Greta directing Will Ferrell on the set of *Barbie* in Venice Beach, California, June 2022.

Entertainment Tonight in 2023. While it's been reported that everyone from Diablo Cody to Amy Schumer had been trying to make a Barbie movie for years, it was only when Margot purchased the rights from Mattel and specifically sought out Greta that the project naturally took shape.

Originally, Greta—known for being a writer-actor-director triple talent—was only supposed to pen the screenplay. But she became so attached to the world she created, and she wanted to fully own it. "I couldn't bear to [let it go]. I had to direct it," she told *Entertainment Tonight*.

In doing so, she completely rewrote the script of the Hollywood summer blockbuster. Warner Bros. had such faith in the project that they allotted a whopping $150 million marketing budget for the film's promotion (more than the $145 million it cost to make). And Mattel agreed not to interfere in the creative process, with CEO Ynon Kreiz giving Greta and Margot his complete blessing—something literally unheard of when millions of dollars and a big reputation are on the line.

Even before it was released, *Barbie* birthed the viral sensation "Barbenheimer," the cheeky moniker merging *Barbie* with *Oppenheimer*, as the two massive summer movies with wildly different perspectives were set to debut on the same weekend. It was a hugely successful phenomenon that drew people back to the movies for the largest weekend after the pandemic. The National Association of Theatre Owners reported a record-breaking two hundred thousand people saw both movies in one day.

There was also the resurgence of the Barbie-core movement—a total commitment to Barbie fashion and the pink aesthetic. After initial promo photos of Margot in the titular role started making the rounds in 2022, searches for "pink clothing" skyrocketed by 416 percent, according to a "Year in Fashion" report from Lyst, as reported on by *Time*. Brands took notice of the trend and capitalized on it in record speed too. Everyone from Xbox to high fashion house Balmain had products to hock; even Airbnb had a real Malibu dreamhouse experience available for rent.

Was it any surprise then that people were in an uproar when the woman at the helm was not recognized for doing the unimaginable

INTRODUCTION 13

and helping resuscitate Hollywood after a lockdown lag by crafting a provocative story about a woman lead? Some wondered if members of the Academy had even seen the film, or if they'd immediately dismissed it on the basis of its supposedly lighter subject matter, especially when pitted against films about the atomic bomb and the Holocaust (*The Zone of Interest*). As the *New York Times* pointed out, the "highbrow group" of Academy member peers who vote on Best Director "are by far the most likely to reject mainstream studio fare."

It's almost like Greta had seen the future when crafting her incredible "never good enough" monologue for America Ferrera's character, Gloria. But if any of it fazed her, Greta didn't let on. She instead saw *Barbie* for the true victory it was. As she told *Time* in their "Women of the Year" profile in early 2024, being nominated for her screenplay was a huge coup itself: "A friend's mom said to me, 'I can't believe you didn't get nominated . . .' I said, 'But I did. I got an Oscar nomination.' She was like, 'Oh, that's wonderful for you!' I was like, 'I know!'"

For Greta, as substantial as *Barbie* was, it was not a bookend to the forty-one-year-old's career or a signal to rest on her laurels. She has plenty more to say and share with her unique vision as a filmmaker, and she's ready to do so with more classic tales like the *Chronicles of Narnia*, upending everything we think we know about these stories. That hallmark will only continue to spellbind, shake up, and transform Hollywood as Greta builds her reputation as a major player in the years to come—a role she was pretty much always born to play.

"I know the right thing, for me anyway, is to keep making movies. Whatever happens, good or bad, you've got to keep going," she said in her conversation with *Time*. "If you love something, you just love it. You don't think to yourself, 'I have to love this because it's by a woman, for a woman.' That's part of it. But it's not why you love it."

Greta on the red carpet for the premiere of Greenberg at the 60th Berlinale Film Festival in Berlin, Germany, February 2010.

Following: Greta attending the EE British Academy Film Awards 2020 at Royal Albert Hall in London, England.

"If you love something,
you just love it.
You don't think to yourself,
'I have to love this because it's
by a woman,
for a woman.'
That's part of it.
But it's not
why you love it."

Greta's World
President Barbie

Of all the detailed characters Greta created for the *Barbie* friendship circle, from Stereotypical Barbie to Weird Barbie, perhaps it was President Barbie that was the most meaningful. In the fictional Barbieland, a woman is in the highest office—at least until Ken discovers patriarchy in the real world and tries to bring her down. Still, President Barbie remains balanced and in support of her fellow dolls when crisis rocks the pink paradise.

The fact that President Barbie is also a Black woman, played by the incredible Issa Rae—who, like Greta, is a director-actress—is another profound development, especially considering that Mattel didn't create the first Black Barbie until 1980, twenty-one years after the first doll was released (as detailed in a recent Netflix documentary). Today, the company has made great strides in being more representative, issuing dolls in all shapes, sizes, and colors.

Greta detailed to the *Guardian* that she was influenced to create the character after touring Mattel's headquarters while working on the script. There, she "saw an image of an all-female Barbie presidential ticket," according to the publication, and the first Barbie POTUS doll which came to market in 1992.

Issa Rae taking on the role of President in *Barbie*, 2023.

"I was like, 'Huh, so Barbie's done it, but we haven't?'" Greta joked to the outlet.

When time came for Issa to find inspiration, she told *Teen Vogue* she turned to "presidential adjacent figures" like Vice President Kamala Harris, Michelle Obama, and German leader Angela Merkel. "But also the childhood version of what I thought a leader would be," she added. "It was tapping into who six- to eight-year-old me thought a female president would look like, and living in that world really informed how I played the president."

Greta and the cast of *Barbie* on the red carpet at the film's world premiere in Los Angeles, California, July 2023.

Opposite: A promotional poster for *Barbie*.

Issa Rae

Barbie

President

Take 1

A Star Is Born

"As a child, my hero was Jo March. But as an adult, it's Louisa May Alcott."

—Greta speaking with the *New York Times* about her undying
love for *Little Women* and its heroines

The year 1983 really left its mark on American culture and entertainment. The Cabbage Patch Dolls made their debut with their unbelievable popularity leading to literal riots. *Flashdance* hit theaters and inspired a generation of leg warmer enthusiasts. KISS shocked everyone after appearing without makeup for the first time on national television. And the Disney Channel premiered, becoming a launching pad for decades of child stars.

It was also the year Greta Celeste Gerwig was born, with her percolating quirky style a seeming birthright that perfectly fit within the timeline of events. Greta's entrance into the world in 1983 also placed her at the tail end of what's become known as the Xennial generation, a crossroads where Gen X and millennials meet on the time

Greta photographed at Schiller's Liquor Bar in New York in 2011.

spectrum. In entertainment speak, it's a finnicky combo audience that's not always easy to find a Venn diagram for, yet it's one that the writer-director-actress has always brilliantly appealed to in equal measure.

Greta's generational universality, in fact, is a big part of the reason why her major directorial debut *Lady Bird* has become such a cult classic, and one that set Greta on the professional path she currently dominates. It's a total mirror for elder '90s kids who, like the title character, grew up with Alanis Morissette, Dave Matthews Band, and Delia's catalogs. Yet when the realistic coming-of-age flick was released in 2017, it was also completely relevant for and resonated with aughts kids too.

The movie's nuanced authenticity is a huge draw, and it all stems from strong similarities to Greta's own formative adolescence. She's been vocal about resisting the term "autobiographical" for her projects, telling *Rolling Stone*, "So many of the things that are personal that come through your movies are never the things that are most obvious to you . . . and that's always part of the joy of making art for people, sometimes they understand it more than you do, which is unsettling." Yet it's hard to ignore the clear parallels, which gave Greta a place of authority to share such a relatable story.

Like Lady Bird, Greta's childhood too was spent in modest Sacramento, California, with a similar middle-class, run-of-the-mill American family who have lived in the same house and who also followed religion, dealt with looming bills, and had a strong nucleus.

Lady Bird's birth name, Christine, is also the name of Greta's mother. Like Laurie Metcalf's character in the film, the real-life Gerwig matriarch is a nurse—an OB-GYN nurse to be exact. And then there's Lady Bird's dad who, in the film, is laid off from being a computer programmer—a job Greta's real dad, Gordon, had early on in his career before he became a small-business loan officer. Greta has a brother and a sister, too, but not much is known about them.

Greta's family—particularly her parents—are real characters, with traits that Greta infuses into nearly every movie, in both literal and figurative ways. There's not just the semi-autobiographical setup of

"That's always part of the **joy** of making **art** for **people**, sometimes they **understand** it more than you do, which is **unsettling.**"

Lady Bird, but also the fact that Greta's own parents played her on-screen parents in *Frances Ha* (when Greta was still early in her career and acting). *Little Women*, too, was largely informed by good parental morals.

As Greta told *Movieguide*, "My mom and dad, they're really good people . . . and I put a lot of that experience of them into this film. It's not sanctimonious morality, but it's real morality, it's real taking care of each other . . . They really have a sense of civic duty in an old-fashioned way . . . a responsibility to take care of the people around you because this is the world we have."

> "When I was a kid, I used to do my homework in the living room, where there was a picture window. And I was hoping that someone would walk by and see me looking very studious."

Greta has often referred to her parents as "hippies," especially in the way they approached raising the Gerwig brood. In a *Gentlewoman UK* interview, she shared that there was no television in their house, save for special occasions: "We had a tiny black-and-white set they kept in a closet and brought out only sometimes." Yet, the absence of regular broadcasts left a gap to fill in with other interests—for Greta, that became a huge love of books, ballet, and theater. In a *New Yorker* article, she explained how her inner thespian showed itself in childhood: "When I was a kid, I used to do my homework in the living room, where there was a picture window. And I was hoping that someone would walk by and see me looking very studious."

The kids weren't allowed to wear logos on any apparel, either, and forget about playing with Barbies—Gordon and Christine didn't, at first, buy their daughter the iconic dolls. But childhood friends started giving Greta their hand-me-downs and she soon became enchanted. "I really do think a big fascination for me was the size of the hair. It was so much hair!" she told *Gentlewoman UK*. Her parents also adopted the liberal '60s-era religion Unitarian Universalism for the family—although, like Lady Bird, Greta was enrolled in a Catholic high school, the all-girls St. Francis.

In high school, Greta's personality and demeanor were nothing like her titular rabble-rouser, who would go as far as to fall out of a moving car to prove her point. "Lady Bird is actually kind of the opposite of how I was," Greta once told *VICE*. "I was a rule-following kind of kid. I never made anybody call me by a different name, I never dyed my hair bright red. But I think, in a way, I was almost creating a heroine that was flawed and could sometimes be a bit of a jerk but also had incredible courage to be herself, even when she was sometimes lying about who she was."

In fact, Greta has gone so far as to call herself an "intense child," explaining to the *Guardian*, "When I loved an activity, I had trouble doing it halfway. It was scary with ballet—I would have gone to class for four hours a day, seven days a week, if I could have." Greta studied ballet for years and was even featured in the Sacramento Ballet's *Nutcracker* for three of them. "I played Clara one year, in fifth grade. I thought that was the pinnacle of my life," she told *Sactown Magazine*.

Yet, she soon had to give up the discipline as she grew and her body didn't fit the ideal ballerina composition. Her mother also thought it was nefarious, especially when Greta's orthodox Royal Ballet teacher wanted to give her a "ballet name": Scarlett. "That put my mom over the edge," Greta told the *Guardian*. "She gave you another name?! No, she can call you by your given name, this is a cult." Sound like a familiar movie scene?

In high school, Christine encouraged Greta to try hip-hop dance. Greta participated for a while in groups called Touch of Style and Fly

Breaking Down Fences

Of all the things Greta tried in her youth—ballet and hip-hop dancing, musical theater, reading, and writing—it's fencing that always throws everyone for a loop. "When I talk about my childhood and then fencing gets thrown in, people are like, 'You've lived so many lives.' But I was very serious about it," Greta told NPR's Terry Gross.

After ballet fell through, as Greta grew older and her body developed, precluding her from continuing with the dance form, she pivoted into the new sport. "My mom read an article that said dancers actually make good fencers because they have good footwork and control, and they're able to shift their weight quickly and move quickly. She signed me up to take a class," she told *Collider*.

Greta soon fell in love with the sport, and fencing actually informed the decision for her to attend a Catholic high school. "The tournaments that I'd have to go to would require me to miss school. And part of the issue was that it was harder at the public school to work around that," she explained to *Collider*. "I took the entrance exam for the Catholic high school, and I talked to Sister Catherine, who was the president of the school at that point, and she said we would be proud to have you represent St. Francis at fencing tournaments, and we would be happy to accommodate whatever school you need to miss."

Eventually, Greta had to give up fencing due to the high expenses of equipment and travel, but she's always held it close to heart. She once gave *Vanity Fair* a look at the moves that made a good fencer in a video interview, ending the clip with, "When you start fencing, you think that you'll look super sexy, taking off your mask, and your hair will flow out. But usually, it's just matted to your head and you're sweaty."

There's also a part of Greta that sees the connection between competitive sports and acting. As she told *Collider*, "There's an economy in sports that I always think is a useful metaphor for acting. You have an objective. You're trying to win, and of course, you want to do well. You want to use good techniques so you enforce it, but also you don't do things you don't have to do." She added, "Using that energy in a scene can really cut the fat off of something and streamline it . . . If you're just wallowing in the emotions of it, then sometimes it doesn't get as clear as when you can just treat it like a fencing match."

Style but abandoned ship pretty quickly. Soon, Greta took up fencing, a sport in which she excelled, once ranking third in the state of California and in the top eight nationally.

The background of it all, like it was in *Lady Bird*, was the dusty California capital of Sacramento, where Greta grew up and also yearned to find her way to New York. As Greta once wrote in a *New York Times* essay, Sacramento is "a place where you can always see the horizon" but the world was fully open in places like NYC. Eventually, life imitated art, with both creator and character successfully making the move to the Big Apple to pursue their dreams.

Part of the draw might have been the Joan Didion effect. One of Greta's great loves has always been books—she's someone who refers to her library as "my dowry" (NPR). As she further shared in an *Interview* conversation, "Books and theater were the way I understood the world, and also the way I organized my sense of morality, of how to live a good life. I would read all night. My mom would come into my room and tell me I had to go to sleep, so I would hide books under my bed." It's easy to see how Greta's love of books has translated to her scripts, which are full of hearty dialogue and wordsmithing. That trait is also a hallmark of the "mumblecore" film style she has long been associated with, a low-budget aesthetic where conversation and relationships reign supreme over plot.

Literature is the springboard from which many of her films materialize too, including her adaptation of Louisa May Alcott's *Little Women* and her upcoming interpretation of *The Chronicles of Narnia*. Even in *Lady Bird*, the movie opens with the title character and her mom listening to *The Grapes of Wrath* audiobook.

So, when Greta realized in her youth that the great novelist and essayist Joan Didion was also from Sacramento, it had a "spiritually seismic" effect, she told *Vanity Fair*. "It was the first time I experienced an artist's eye looking at my home. I had always thought art and writing had to be about things that were 'important,' and I was certain that my life was not at all important. But her writing, so beautiful and clear and

"Books and theater were the way I understood the world, and also the way I organized my sense of morality, of how to live a good life."

"I never made anybody call me by a different name. I never dyed my hair bright red. But I think, in a way, I was almost creating a heroine that was flawed and could sometimes be a bit of a jerk but also had incredible courage to be herself . . ."

specific, was about *my* world." In Greta's list of her ten all-time favorite books for *Vulture*, a list that includes titles by Virginia Woolf, Alice Munro, and George Eliot, she also includes Joan's *The White Album*, calling the author "my patron saint."

In *Lady Bird*, Greta pays homage to the writer by displaying one of her great quotes on the screen in the opening moments: "Anybody who talks about California hedonism has never spent a Christmas in Sacramento." Joan too escaped the California "cow town" to head to the more glamorous New York City, perhaps setting the mold and example for both Greta and Lady Bird to follow as well.

Though she eventually put down roots elsewhere, Greta has frequently called *Lady Bird* her "love letter to Sacramento." As she explained to the Associated Press in 2017, "I wanted to set it in Sacramento because Sacramento is my hometown and I love it and I thought I could shoot it lovingly." She added, "I'm a big believer in the more specific you make something the more universal it is, and because it's about this core feeling of how you can't understand how much you love home until you're leaving it, everyone would think about their hometown and their particular geography of their childhood and how they relate to that as an adult."

In interviews, Greta has shown that same 20/20 hindsight appreciation more than once, often waxing ecstatic about how her upbringing molded her and how the creature comforts of home enthralled her. She even came to love the agriculture facets that Lady Bird despised. "The State Fair was a huge thing for me. I loved the livestock competitions," Greta told local paper the *Sacramento Bee*. "There was always a cow that was about to give birth and it always took sooo long, and you'd just keep checking back."

There were also the theaters of Sacramento's Midtown, another favorite topic of conversation. "The New Helvetia Theatre. I loved that theater. The 24th Street Theater. The Memorial Auditorium? And the little theater off to the side of the Memorial Auditorium?" she shared with the *Bee*.

Greta with Saoirse Ronan on the set of 2017 film *Lady Bird*.

"I'm a big believer in the more specific you make something the more universal it is."

In addition to books and ballet, Greta has always loved musicals and show tunes, and she was encouraged as a child to see productions and become involved in community theater. "I don't think people think of Sacramento necessarily as a place where you can see a lot of theater, but there is a lot of great community theater there. I was seeing one or two plays a week, every week, for my entire childhood," she told *Bust* magazine.

In fact, it was the plays that she read before literature that would shape her own writing style. As she told Francis Ford Coppola in an artist-on-artist chat in *Interview* magazine, "At first I had a tough time getting through novels, so I read plays, because a play is generally

Greta on the *Lady Bird* set in 2017, dressing the part while filming the prom scene.

shorter and has all those tools for getting people hooked early on." When she was a child, Greta would also write her own short productions and cast her family to act in them, like a little Jo March.

As she's gotten older and advanced in her career, Greta has also had a curious understanding for how theater productions translate to the big screen—heck, she's even cast the playwright Tracy Letts in *Lady Bird* and *Little Women*, a nod to her great appreciation for the synergy between the two. *Singin' in the Rain* is one of her favorite movies, as she told ABC10 Morning News' Mark S. Allen. "All those soundstage musicals like *Singin' in the Rain* and *An American in Paris* and *Oklahoma* and *Gigi* and *Meet Me in St. Louis*, these were all movies that I just loved and they have this kind of glorious, I call it authentic artificiality with beautiful painted skies and in camera builds," she explained, "it's just so gorgeous." In fact, she took many of those cues for *Barbie*, adapting them into her similar pink paradise soundstages. The "I'm Just Ken" ballet escapade—that too was based on the dream ballet from *Singin' in the Rain*.

Thanks to the influence of musicals, Greta believed for a while that she wanted to be a nun, laughably, not only "because of the way they dressed," she told ABC10 Morning News, but also because "they had a musical, *The Sound of Music*. And I thought, you know, I would enjoy being a nun in *The Sound of Music*."

In the Catholic school system, Greta got her fair share of exposure to women in habits. She also knew plenty of religious scriptures, with her love for prose and story beginning with the Bible itself. "I think I always go back to those older story forms because I went to Catholic school and I resonate with them," she told the Associated Press of her attachment to ancient biblical tales.

Most of her movies feature some kind of religious symbolism and

Greta at the Film Independent Spirit Awards Show, accepting the win for Best Screenplay for *Lady Bird*, March 2018.

Following: Greta in a still from the 2012 film *Lola Versus*.

A STAR IS BORN

"What I do now feels the closest to being a kid that I've ever been. I get to kind of create these imaginary worlds and live inside them, and that feels basically what it was like when I was playing make believe on the playground."

innocent, irreverent fun, like making Lady Bird's given name Christine (a nod not only to Greta's mom but also a "female version of Christ"), decorating the head nun's minivan with "Just Married to Jesus" paraphernalia in *Lady Bird*, and references to the Sistine Chapel and its iconic ceiling artwork of God touching Adam's hand in some of the *Barbie* scenes. However, for that final reference point, she turned the archetype into a feminist moment, with Mattel founder Ruth Handler touching hands with Margot Robbie's Barbie in a pivotal moment alluding to creator and creation.

Greta admits that she has never been devout with any religion, but has always found the traditions important and thinks of them as their own kind of muse in her art. "I don't have an identity or affiliation with a particular institution. But the ritual of religion is something I really love and I'm really drawn to, whether it's the Catholic traditions or the Protestant traditions," she told *VICE*. "I've gone with my friends to mosque and to synagogues and all of that is something I find very moving and true. There's something about it that I always feel connects us to our deepest need for storytelling."

Even though Greta nicknamed her fictional *Lady Bird* high school "Immaculate Fart," it's clear she's still in good standing with her real alma mater. St. Francis Catholic High School not only hosted an Oscar party when *Lady Bird* was nominated in 2018, but it also proudly lists her as a 2002 alumnus on their website: "While at SF, Greta was part of the Dance program, Chamber Choir, and numerous theatre productions," the school shares. St. Francis also lists the various theatrical productions that Greta was involved in during her time there, charting a clear throughline from her days as a child watching Hollywood musicals to her work in the present day. Among the productions she took part in are *Into the Woods*, *The Boy Friend*, *Pippin*, and *The Apple Tree*.

While at St. Francis, Greta also took part in the Lenaea High School

Greta with actor Jesse Eisenberg in a still from the 2012 film *To Rome With Love*.

Theatre Festival, described on their website as "an annual three-day educational event at which high school students come together to perform theatrical pieces, receive evaluation and feedback from theatre professionals, and attend workshops on theatre topics." St. Francis notes that Greta participated in Lenaea performances of *Antigone*, *Final Dress Rehearsal*, and *Ladies of the Tower*; for *Ladies*, Greta was a festival medalist.

This love of the stage soon called Greta to New York, where she fully intended to become a musical theater major. Yet all the dominoes would soon fall another way, into a career that has endured since the 2010s and lives up to her wildest childhood dreams. "What I do now feels the closest to being a kid that I've ever been," she told ABC10 News. "I get to kind of create these imaginary worlds and live inside them, and that feels basically what it was like when I was playing make believe on the playground at [elementary school] Phoebe Hearst."

Greta in a still from the 2012 film *Lola Versus*.

Opposite: Greta in the 2012 film *Lola Versus*.

Greta's World
Lady Bird

Greta Gerwig has never been a director in the Hitchcock vein by inserting herself into her films in obvious ways. But she did so more subtly and beautifully with the character of Lady Bird, a thrift-store-loving, theater-immersed, coffeeshop-working teen with a sharp tongue and an inquisitive mind.

Greta's first major film was semi-autobiographical, with all the hallmarks of the people, places, and things that populated her childhood in Sacramento in the 1990s and 2000s, and there were many traits of her own being that filtered into the title character. But with Lady Bird, she also had the chance to revise her own history. Greta has admitted that she was never as bold or brazen as Lady Bird in her youth—she probably would have been caught dead before she was found eating unconsecrated communion wafers or caught in a lie about the house she lived in.

"I think some of her mouthiness was what I would maybe think in my head, but not actually say. Her boldness, really. Her going after what she wants, even with romantic interests, she didn't wait for anybody to notice her. She was gonna really go after what she wanted and who she was into," Greta shared with *VICE*. "I admire that and I wish I had been more like that."

Saoirse Ronan in a still from 2017 film *Lady Bird*.

A STAR IS BORN

Take 2

Behind the Scenes

"It felt a universe away from the kids-on-bikes town that was Sacramento. It seemed impossible that it was the same country. And yet somehow, it also felt like home."

—Greta in an essay for the *New York Times* about becoming an adoptee of NYC

Many a creative mind has waxed ecstatic about New York City. Frank Sinatra said if he could make it there, he could make it anywhere. Truman Capote believed, "New York is not a city, it's a world." Greta's writer idol Joan Didion also had some thoughts: "I still believed in possibilities . . . still had the sense, so peculiar to New York, that something extraordinary would happen any minute, any day, any month."

Yet it was actually an essay from *Charlotte's Web* writer E. B. White, called "Here Is New York," that first kick-started Greta's "mythological"

Greta on the set of the 2011 film *Arthur*.

47

fascination with the city, as she relayed to *Variety*. In particular, it was the line that reads, "No one should move to New York unless he's willing to be lucky."

And so, wide-eyed and full of possibility, nineteen-year-old Greta followed in the footsteps of the many greats before her, making the inspired journey in 2002 to the city that never sleeps. Judging by her list of credits during this time—twenty-five roles in films and five co-writing credits before even making her big debut with *Lady Bird*—she probably didn't get much sleep herself. Lady Bird would've been proud. Greta accomplished their shared dream, finding her way out of Sac-Town after falling for NYC's women's liberal arts institution Barnard College and thrusting herself into the booming metropolis where all dreams were possible.

"I felt 'Ah, yes, now life can really begin,' as if life hadn't been going on before," Greta shared of her initiation to the city in a beautiful 2018 essay for the *New York Times*. The piece is full of the explicitly detailed prose that would later come to dominate her scripts: "Against explicit warnings not to, I climbed to the roof of my dorm to look down at the city below," she wrote. "It was my city, or I wanted it to be. But I had no idea which way was uptown and which was downtown. This place I had wanted so badly to be part of was still a mystery."

New York was not exactly foreign to Greta, however. The family had visited the city on more than one occasion when Greta and her siblings were young, and it left an indelible impression on the young talent, particularly seeing all the Broadway shows that fostered an early love of the theater. "When we waited for hours to get rush tickets . . . Mom befriended people in line . . . they became very invested in the little blond girl getting in to see the show. And I did: *42nd Street* with Jerry Orbach. *Gypsy* with Tyne Daly. *Cats* with cats," Greta shared in her essay.

There were some familial roots too. In that same loving *NYT* tribute, entitled, "My Mother, My City," Greta reveals that "I Love NY" was not just a silly catchphrase for the Gerwig women; the sentiment

"I instantly saw **five girls** who I thought I want to be them . . . they seemed like **superheroes** to me."

The Best and Brightest of Barnard College

Greta graduated from New York's Barnard College in 2006 and earned her spot among the notable alumni from this renowned women's liberal arts institution. From actresses to Congresspeople, Greta was in perfect company within the Barnard sisterhood. Looking at this list of other revolutionaries, it's no wonder that the first time she walked onto the campus, Greta knew she wanted to be like all the other women around her.

ERINN SMART (class of 2001): An Olympian, Erinn competed as part of the US fencing team and took home the silver medal in the 2008 Beijing games.

EDWIDGE DANTICAT (class of 1990): The Haitian-American writer is a Pushcart Short Story Prize winner and National Book Critics Circle Award recipient. Her title *Breath, Eyes, Memory* was notably an Oprah's Book Club pick in 1998.

DELIA EPHRON (class of 1966): The beloved author and screenwriter behind classic films like *You've Got Mail* and *The Sisterhood of the Traveling Pants*.

LAUREN GRAHAM (class of 1988): Perhaps best known as the quick-witted Lorelai Gilmore of *Gilmore Girls*, the actress also appeared on the shows *Parenthood* and *Zoey's Extraordinary Playlist* and in movies like *Bad Santa* and *Evan Almighty*.

ALEX GUARNASCHELLI (class of 1991): One of the most recognizable foodies, Alex has appeared on a cooking shows like *The Kitchen, Chopped, Iron Chef America,* and *Alex vs. America.*

CYNTHIA NIXON (class of 1988): The *Sex and the City* star won an Emmy for her role as Miranda Hobbes well as Tony awards for her work on Broadway.

CHELSEA PERETTI (class of 2000): The funny gal is best known for her comedic chops on the show *Brooklyn Nine-Nine* as well as being a featured writer on *Parks and Recreation.*

MARTHA STEWART (class of 1963): The home décor guru, cooking diva, and all around hostess with the mostest is a proud Barnard College alum.

TWYLA THARP (class of 1963): The renowned dancer and choreographer behind works like the ballet crossover *Push Comes To Shove, Deuce Coupe,* and the Broadway musical *Movin' Out.*

HELEN GAHAGAN DOUGLAS (class of 1924): Helen led a remarkable life, acting on Broadway and the silver screen in the Golden Age of Hollywood. But perhaps she's most regarded for being the first Democrat woman elected to the US Congress in 1944.

BEHIND THE SCENES

was embedded in their DNA. "The first New Yorker I ever knew was my mother, Chris Gerwig," Greta explained, going on to describe how the matriarch grew up in Brooklyn as a small child. "She had and has the spirit of a quintessential New York City gal. She's brash and smart and tough and funny . . . She was in her element . . . So was I. The Gerwig women belonged in New York."

Greta followed that destiny. At first, she journeyed to the Big Apple to try out for the musical theater programs at NYU and Juilliard, believing the musicals she always loved were in the cards for her. As fate would have it, Greta was not accepted into either program. Her mother, who wasn't necessarily sold on her daughter's stage ambitions, seemed pleased with the outcome. As Greta told the *Guardian*: "She said, 'I'm not spending $40,000 a year for you to learn how to tap dance.'"

Her father, Gordon, was a bit more enthused. He instead joined Greta on the trip, and upon the rejections from NYU and Juilliard, he pushed his daughter to look into Columbia University and its affiliated school Barnard College, a private women's liberal arts institute founded in 1889 as one of the original Seven Sisters schools. "I said absolutely not, I don't want to . . . I thought I definitely wanted to be in a conservatory setting, I didn't want to go to a traditional college," Greta told *CBS Sunday Morning*. But, after more prodding from her father, she gave Barnard a shot and soon felt at home, adding, "I instantly saw five girls who I thought I want to be them . . . they seemed like superheroes to me."

At Barnard, Greta was in the good company of the many heroines who had come before her. Among the alumni who found their footing at the college were actresses Cynthia Nixon and Lauren Graham, musician Laurie Anderson, author Zora Neale Hurston, even Joan Rivers and Martha Stewart. Greta, class of 2006, majored in English (with, of course, a theater concentration). She also studied philosophy and was on the debate team for a while, all funded via scholarships and loans.

Several of her professors have since commented on what a diligent learner and bright mind Greta was at the time. "She was so intellectually curious. She was so remarkably creative. And she just wanted to sample so much," Patricia Denison, Greta's faculty adviser, commented in a post on Barnard's website. "She wrote wonderful essays and was a standout in class discussions, taking our conversations to higher planes while keeping a sense of humor and earning the affection of her classmates . . . the class was simply better because she was in it," added English professor Peter Platt.

Studying in Barnard's English program was a game changer in the development of the Greta Gerwig that has come into our cultural consciousness in the past few decades. It was here where her writing became her main mode of artistic exploration. But the seed had been planted years prior, when she was in the eighth grade at Phoebe Hearst Elementary, as Greta explained to the *New York Times*. She first knew she was a "writer with a capital W" after scribing a story for a school literary journal about a girl who pees her pants and a female classmate who helps her. It was not only accepted into the publication but also hung on the board at the school by a teacher who loved it.

That tale, like so many others from Greta's fictional world, was based off of a personal experience (she really did have a classroom accident and a classmate did come to her rescue with a sweatshirt to tie around her waist). "I knew in it there was a story that was funny and sweet," she told the *New York Times*. This pivotal moment is what has long become the brand of Greta Gerwig and her pantheon of original scripts (and

"It was the first movie I saw that it really clicked, like: Oh, there is a language and a grammar that is specific to film, that is its own."

BEHIND THE SCENES 53

"I didn't even know who made films when I was growing up. I used to think that films were sort of handed down from gods."

some of the adapted ones too): finding the heart in life's challenges, the profundity in its most trivial moments, and, at the center of it all, the unmistakable bond of women who help each other out.

Or, as the *New York Times* asserts of that early piece of writing, "In Gerwig's hands, the story is not primarily about shame, and it is decidedly not about adolescent cruelty or the whispers of gossip. It's a generous, goofy story about a pratfall, and a meta-story about making a certain kind of art out of life—an art steeped in female reciprocity and resilience."

While Greta's elementary and Catholic high school years may have given her an endless amount of material for her later works, it was perhaps the experimental playground and feminine energy of Barnard that really influenced Greta and gave her carte blanche to make such creative and risk-taking movies in the years that followed. As her adviser Patricia summarized, "In the English Department, you have an emphasis on doing a tremendous amount of reading as well as [on] a tremendous amount of writing, so the best creative writers are also doing analytical writing and then they can begin to focus on a particular genre. So they can really try out different ways of being a writer."

And did she ever. During her college years, Greta was already starting to show her prolific writing side, mostly homing in on playwriting, which merged her loves of theater and prose. It was all thanks to the encouragement of her teachers who applauded the original pieces Greta crafted. "It sounds so silly. It just really never occurred to me that I could do it," she told the *Gentlewoman UK*. But she was actually quite good at it. As the *New York Times* summarizes of two examples, "One play she wrote featured a seduction scene in which someone breaks a jar of mayonnaise onstage. Another one, which involved a daughter murdering her mother, was written in two weeks' time, after a group lost the rights to perform 'Misery.'"

Based on the 1987 thriller written by Stephen King, *Misery* was also adapted into a film released in 1990 and a play by Simon Moore in 1992,

BEHIND THE SCENES

all of which Greta loved—a perfect example of the dual interpretations that started giving her ideas for how the page could develop onto the stage or screen. In her interview with *Gentlewoman UK*, Greta shared, "I had grown up loving theatre so much, and a lot of the films that I also loved were often adaptations of plays . . . where the filmmaking's extraordinary but the language is also language." The 1999 war drama *Beau Travail* was incredibly provocative for Greta in this regard. She said, "It was the first movie I saw that it really clicked, like: Oh, there is a language and a grammar that is specific to film, that is its own."

As a *New York Times* profile further elaborates, during her time at Barnard, Greta started to become more aware of film as art. She was a frequent customer at a boutique video store called Kim's, where she'd rent countless titles. Again, in this article, *Beau Travail* comes up as a turning point, yet for a different reason: "[Greta] didn't realize until she saw Claire Denis's name in the credits that it had been directed by a woman. She remembers thinking: That's a job you can have?"

"I didn't even know who made films when I was growing up," she once confessed to *Dazed* magazine. "I used to think that films were sort of handed down from gods."

Film also showed her another way to take a character off the page and breathe life into it—and it was a form of expression she was eager to try. And so, when she was still in college, Greta began her first venture into acting, using Barnard's connections with Columbia to take specialty courses and also joining the university's Varsity Show for two terms, from 2003 to 2005. One of her castmates (and brief dormmate) just happened to be actress/comic and *Saturday Night Live* alumnus Kate McKinnon. "She was always the most talented person I knew and that still holds true," Greta told *People*. The two also had an improv group together, where Greta's writing skills came into focus yet again.

Greta with friend and former college dormmate Kate McKinnon plus America Ferrera and Michael Cera at a *Barbie* event.

GRETA

"Weird" Beginnings with Kate McKinnon

Long before Greta cast Kate McKinnon to play Weird Barbie in her 2023 blockbuster film, the two talents were living and working together at Columbia/Barnard in the early 2000s while involved in the university's Varsity Show. They also had their own side project, an improv troupe called the Tea Party.

"It was before the [political] Tea Party," Greta joked with *Yahoo*. "[Kate and I] got rejected from the main improv group. So then we started our own . . . and would hold our shows at the exact same time so that people would have to choose who they wanted to be friends with more. It was hilarious." Calling what they came up with "wonderfully strange musicals," Greta added in a *People* interview, "We were thinking like, 'I hope someone will wanna work with us one day, . . . In some ways, hopefully we've grown and changed and developed as artists and in other ways we're doing exactly what we were doing at nineteen."

Both talents of course have gone on to great success, with many people wanting to work with them, but they've still found ways to work together too. Greta has appeared on *Saturday Night Live* in two small bits, once in 2017 when *Lady Bird* actress Saoirse Ronan hosted and Greta appeared as a boss lady in a digital short called "The Race," and again in 2023, when Greta popped up alongside Kate as the latter hosted for the first time, to help introduce Billie Eilish as she sang the *Barbie* song, "What Was I Made For?"

In approaching Kate for the role of Weird Barbie, Greta recalled to *60 Minutes* how their initial conversation went when pitching the idea. "I said, 'You know those Barbies you play with way too much and you cut their hair and you draw on them?' And she said, 'Yes. That's all I had. And my cat peed on them.' And I said, 'That's right. Exactly. *That* Barbie.' And she's like, 'I could not want to do something more.'"

While Greta has called Kate "the most talented person," Kate has also had loving things to say about Greta. "She's one of the smartest people you could meet in the universe and also . . . the enthusiasm," Kate told *Elle* in a promo video for *Barbie*. "I was like, how is she managing to muster this much genuine passion for every single millimeter of everything that's going on?"

Kate McKinnon as Weird Barbie in a still from the 2023 movie.

BEHIND THE SCENES

With her time at Barnard wrapping up, Greta focused in on her playwriting. A bio for one of her films, *Hannah Takes The Stairs*, notes she was a "writer-in-residence at the Vassar College and New York Stage & Film's Powerhouse Theater Festival" during the summer of 2006. At the time, she also applied to several MFA graduate programs around New York. "I got rejected from every graduate school I applied to," Greta shared during an appearance on the *Employee of the Month* podcast in 2016, noting she had once again applied to NYU, Juilliard, and even Yale. "I just got like a universal, 'No thanks.'"

Even working as a more developed, in-demand writer in Hollywood now, Greta still thinks the primitive script she submitted with her MFA application was quite good. "I recently went back and read the play that I had submitted and I thought I was going to have that thing where you look back at something you wrote and you think, 'Oh this was terrible. I understand.' And I still thought it was pretty good," she said on *Employee of the Month*. "It was a play about Kant and Newton as thirteen-year-old boys trying to date girls and debating the nature of space, and it's really funny. I don't know, I think they made a mistake."

Of course, this was not the first time Greta had dealt with rejection, and by now she knew how to pick herself up and find her next steps forward. Soon, the budding talent was switching gears again, dabbling more in the world of acting, though this time, within the world of indie film. "I felt that theatre was closed, but that when it came to film, the door was very slightly ajar. If I have any virtues, it's that I'm good at walking through doors that are slightly ajar," she told the *Guardian*. It was yet another pivotal turn that would eventually lead her to the Hollywood big leagues, though not before she'd suffered a bit for her art.

As Greta told *Time Out* of her post-collegiate years, "I lived for two years with six girls in an apartment that was built for three people, and it had no heat. We would sleep in our coats and in sleeping bags." She was also taking odd jobs as an SAT tutor and sometimes nanny. Still, she wouldn't have had it any other way, recalling in the article, "Once a day I had a feeling of, 'I can't believe I live here.' I'm so lucky." Living in

"If I have any **virtues,** it's that **I'm good** at walking through **doors** that are slightly **ajar.**"

"I'm interested in other people. It's one of the reasons I like living in New York City. I like seeing people, running into people. I wouldn't do well alone in the woods."

New York also gave her endless opportunities for innocent voyeurism, where she could pick up bits and pieces of all the humans she came into contact with, giving her all kinds of personalities to bring into the worlds she wrote. "I'm interested in other people. It's one of the reasons I like living in New York City. I like seeing people, running into people. I wouldn't do well alone in the woods," she told the *Guardian*.

Greta's first acting opportunity came with the indie flick *LOL*, directed by a once unknown Midwesterner named Joe Swanberg. The connection came through one of Greta's college boyfriends, who said his pal Joe needed people to offer up selfies and voice messages for a no-budget film he was working on about chat rooms (remember, this was 2006). Greta obliged, playing basically herself, and soon after, director Joe was asking if she wanted to be involved in his next project, the beloved coming-of-age cult classic *Hannah Takes The Stairs*, for which Greta also received her first official writing credit on a film.

Taking part in the project involved moving to Chicago—Joe's home—for a summer and Greta willingly signed on. Yet again, her instincts paid off. During filming, she holed up in a rental property with a squad of housemates that were also on the cusp of breaking out, including actor Mark Duplass (currently on *The Morning Show*), indie director/screenwriter Andrew Bujalski (often regarded as the "godfather of mumblecore," the genre Greta would soon become

Greta celebrating the 2011 film *No Strings Attached* at the Tribeca Grand Hotel in New York.

 GRETA

"It can be very **hard** to get in the **front doors,** so **building** these sort of **side-communities** of **filmmakers** or **writers** or **actors** is **important.**"

associated with), and multi-talented Kent Osborne who went on to be a prominent figure in the animated TV world.

Through these early connections, Greta also later met Josh and Benny Safdie (the brothers behind movies like *Good Time* and *Uncut Gems*), horror giant Ti West (creator of the *X-Pearl-MaXXXine* trilogy), even Lena Dunham of *Girls* fame. They started to coalesce into a small indie scene, entering their films into modest festivals (including a substantial trip to SXSW in Austin, Texas), and all working together for the greater good of their art.

"I found my group. I found a group of artists that took my work seriously, and I took their work seriously. And nobody was making a living doing it, but we all held each other to a standard of seriousness, which I think is almost more valuable than being accepted by the powers," Greta told *Dazed* magazine of that formative group of creatives whose passion pushed them forward. "It can be very hard to get in the front doors, so building these sort of side-communities of filmmakers or writers or actors is important."

Low-budget movie sets were also Greta's trial by fire. After graduating with an English degree from Barnard and being rejected for all those MFA programs, Greta chose experiential learning over the classroom as her way forward. "I've wanted to be a writer-director for a long time but because I didn't go to film school, I sort of did it on set," she told Jimmy Fallon in an appearance on his late-night show. "When I was acting or co-writing or producing, I was figuring out how you get a movie from [the] page to it being released." That included everything from holding a boom mic to applying makeup.

Much of this foundational early part of Greta's career post-college was really a matter of right place, right time, and finding an environment that fostered the indie, DIY spirit, in which she and her contemporaries were able to make art. During the early 2000s, New York City was still coming out of the shadows of the horrific events of the 9/11 terrorist attacks and trying to find its identity again, including reinvigorating its reputation as a cultural hub.

BEHIND THE SCENES

"The prospect of anyone giving me enough of a paycheck where I could have health insurance and pay my rent, that was very appealing. But, looking back, it never felt right, it wasn't my path. I don't exactly know what I am. But I'm not a well-known mainstream actor who does studio films."

"In the early 2000s, New York City's economic landscape created a world in which one could survive off of little. Artists, skaters, graffiti writers, poets and musicians inhabited the city, organically creating style and culture in a way that permeated into the life of the neighborhood," said *Living Proof*, in an article about photographer Alain Levitt's book *New York: 2000–2005*. "Downtown New York housed a thriving underground scene flourishing amongst a mixture of partying and youth in a carefree time of unhindered creativity."

In the film world, indie entities like the Tribeca Film Fest were starting to crop up, too, providing a more substantial platform for DIY filmmakers. The annual event was founded in 2001 by actor Robert De Niro and partners Jane Rosenthal and Craig Hatkoff "to spur the economic and cultural revitalization of lower Manhattan following the attacks on the World Trade Center," according to the festival's official website. Greta and her growing posse took part in several iterations of the event, notably in 2012 when *Lola Versus* was screened in its world premiere; in the film, Greta took on the title role.

Yet even though Greta was starting to amass recognition in acting circles, it still didn't feel right to her. "I didn't know what I was doing," she told the *Guardian* in 2015 about those early acting gigs. She already sensed there was a different course that would lead her to becoming a true auteur. "The prospect of anyone giving me enough of a paycheck where I could have health insurance and pay my rent, that was very appealing. But, looking back, it never felt right, it wasn't my path. I don't exactly know what I am. But I'm not a well-known mainstream actor who does studio films."

Greta at the Academy Museum of Motion Pictures 3rd Annual Gala, December 2023.

BEHIND THE SCENES

Greta's World
Jo March

So much of Greta Gerwig's approach for character development in her original scripts can really be seen as revisionist feminist fantasy, whether it's remaking her own self (wanting to have been as blunt and bold as teenage Lady Bird) or the events of history itself (giving the dream land in *Barbie* a female president). Even in her adapted works, Greta finds an incredible spin that makes viewers rethink their own ideology or association with an enduring female character. This is especially the case when it comes to Josephine "Jo" March.

In her 2019 take on *Little Women,* Greta gives viewers an ending not in the book. In Louisa May Alcott's classic novel, Jo marries Professor Friedrich Bhaer, eschewing the forward-thinking ideals she hereto had about marriage (reducing it to an "economic proposal") and the belief that women were able to remain independent. In Greta's version, we get two parallels for the female lead. Yes, there's Jo ending up with Friedrich and frolicking with children at the site of her newly opened school in a scene of domestic bliss. But there's also a flip of the switch, one that counters publisher Robert Brothers' belief that a female lead must end up married or dead by the end of a novel, a perspective that has never sat well with Greta. As she once told *Bust,* "I've consciously tried to write female characters where their central story is not a question of whether she will or will not end up with some dude"—and that certainly applies to her approach in *Little Women.*

Saoirse Ronan as Jo March in a still from Greta's 2019 film, *Little Women.*

BEHIND THE SCENES 69

As the movie pans out from the scenes depicting Jo's married life, the film ends with Jo embracing her freshly bound finished novel. It's enough to leave the viewer with the idea that the leading lady gets her true happy ending—writing her book. "Kind of the hat trick I wanted to pull off was, what if you felt, when she gets her book, the way you generally feel about a girl getting kissed? What if we could figure out how to do that?" Greta relayed to *Vanity Fair*. "So it's not girl gets boy, [it's] girl gets book."

Of course, *Little Women* was originally written by Louisa May Alcott in 1868, light years ahead of the women's suffrage movement and women's lib, developments that gave women the rights to vote and to have property outside of their husbands, which was not the case for the March sisters or for the author herself. Today, women can be single and independent, or they can be mothers and wives and also have their own careers and ambitions, a balance that Greta has found in her own life. Even so, you have to sense that there's a bit of Jo March in her: Not only are they both writers who love the theater, but also when the film opens on Jo living and thriving in New York, ready to present her writing ideas to a big, ostentatious publisher, it's also a bit of art imitating life.

Greta and actress Saoirse Ronan on the set of the 2019 film *Little Women*, shot on location in Massachusetts.

Following: Greta directing her *Little Women* cast, including Florence Pugh, Emma Watson, and Saoirse Ronan, Massachusetts, 2019.

Take 3

In Front of the Camera

"I love getting passports, because when you get a passport,
it expires in ten years, and you have this physical object, and you think,
'What are the next ten years going to hold?'"

—Greta in a 2018 interview with *Bust* magazine

The decade between Greta Gerwig's onscreen debut in 2006's *LOL* and her major directorial debut with 2017's *Lady Bird* is perhaps one of the most fascinating in the timeline of her artistic developments.

During this span, Greta tried out acting and quickly became an indie star darling, but at the same time, she brilliantly reframed her experience on low-budget film sets to take in everything she needed to know to make her own movies in the future. She started writing more screenplays, with the likes of Joe Swanberg and Noah Baumbach (whom she would also become romantically linked with), and thus,

Greta posing on the beach for a portrait during the Sarasota Film Festival in Florida, April 2007.

started developing her first true collaborations, which would become huge parts of the community she built around her in future projects. And she also started becoming obsessed with the idea of directing, particularly intent on finding a woman's place in Hollywood's notorious boys' club.

These experiences would shape her into the dynamic moviemaker that all but broke the mold in Tinseltown, a figure heralded on Medium as "Hollywood's girl on fire," someone "leading by example" (*Time*), and "the brain behind *Barbie*" (*Rolling Stone*), among other high marks.

But in 2009, after getting her first taste of cinema in *LOL*, *Hannah Takes the Stairs*, *Baghead*, *Yeast*, and *Nights and Weekends*, Greta and her filmmaking buddy Joe Swanberg were simply the "penny-pinching future of indie cinema," according to *Paste* magazine. Putting the duo on the cover, *Paste* offered an exposé about the new school style of filmmaking, with Joe and Greta at the helm of a "slew of talented, original directors who have thrived despite—and sometimes because of—zero budgets and improvised means."

Greta and Joe Swanberg in a still from the 2008 film *Nights and Weekends*.

TUMBLING INTO MUMBLECORE

This DIY style became its own burgeoning genre known as mumblecore, for which Greta is often considered one of the poster children. The ethos is to get as close to real-life as possible: improvised lines, friends and other non-actor randoms dominating the cast, actual apartments as sets, and shaky filmmaking with the use of handheld cameras from Best Buy. Rather than thick plot, obvious props, and gimmicky special effects, mumblecore films also focused on dialogue, character development, and the intricate workings of various relationships. At the core was "naturalism" and "personal/confessional" stories, per *MasterClass*, that zeroed in on the types of daily interactions you could expect in real-life, with the moviemakers typically "mak[ing] films about themselves and their friends' lives." And as it turns out, we may have reality TV to thank for it.

"The threat of the actors' strike in 2001 that paved the way for a lot of reality TV to hit the mainstream made a huge impact on the way mass audiences perceived handheld video," Joe Swanberg told *Paste*. "Because they got used to watching it, all in one year, with *Survivor* and every other show that came along shot in a run-and-gun style on a small camera." He added, "This whole idea of exposing very personal inner thoughts to a general public whether they wanted it or not seemed really crazy five years ago. But it was around the same time that these smaller movies started to do something similar . . . I made my first two movies for less than three thousand bucks."

For Greta, it was a style that spring-boarded from her experiences in improv with Columbia's Varsity Show and her Tea Party troupe with Kate McKinnon. In the lead role in the 2007 flick *Hannah Takes the Stairs*, Greta shined as the "neurotic, sweet and mildly sarcastic" (*New York Times*) title character who, while working as a production intern, finds herself in a lovers' tangle with her boyfriend while also developing feelings for two coworkers. As the newspaper hailed, Greta comes off as a "Gen Y-Diane Keaton." The *New York Observer* went so far as to brand her "mumblecore's Meryl Streep." Notably, *Hannah*

IN FRONT OF THE CAMERA

Greta and Mark Duplass on the set of the 2007 movie *Hannah Takes the Stairs*.

Takes the Stairs also marked Greta's first official writing credit on a film.

A year later, in 2008, Greta starred in Jay and Mark Duplass' horror-comedy romp *Baghead* as Michelle, one of four hopeful actors who retire to a cabin in the woods to write a script, where things go awry. The *Los Angeles Times* said of Greta's performance, "The character is by turns flighty and wily, determined to get what she wants even if she doesn't always know what that is, and [it] provides an ideal launchpad for Gerwig's distinctively natural, goofy-yet-sultry screen presence."

Also in 2008 was *Nights and Weekends*, for which Greta wrote the script with Joe Swanberg. She also directed and produced for the first time on that film, and starred in it, too, playing Mattie, who's involved in a long-distance relationship with James (played by Joe). Viewers watch their relationship start to spiral and dissolve. At the time, Joe and Greta's own working relationship was becoming fractured, as she told *Vulture*, and they were fighting a lot. Soon enough, she'd leave that working relationship behind and venture into new and non-mumblecore territory.

That categorical name has actually become one that Greta has grown to loathe. "It's the worst term. I hate it. I think anyone who made those movies and then has to hear that term hates that term. I'm just waiting for the day that I never have to hear it again," Greta told the *Hollywood Reporter* in 2016 about being lumped into the mumblecore milieu. And while she admitted to the *Guardian*, "I'm so grateful for the experience," she also joked, "All the early movies I made, I literally can't look at them . . . I get motion sickness." And really, Greta was much more interested in developing a bona fide script that could be seen "as a piece of writing . . . as opposed to just shooting improv and finding the film in the edit."

Yet, there are so many mumblecore hallmarks that Greta clearly liked and took with her into her later projects. A focus on dialogue? Check. Less plot and more looking at relationships? Check. The exploration of natural, real-life dichotomies? Check.

But 2008 wasn't her time to start making headway with her own projects. Back then, Greta was just struggling to get by. As she told the *Guardian*, "I was really depressed. I cried a lot. It was a hard year. I was twenty-five and thinking, 'This is supposed to be the best time and I'm miserable.'" Looking back at that era of her life, she added, "I wish I had taken that time and written more, but it felt like acting was happening for me, and I went back to acting classes. The blessing and curse of my life is that I think I thrive when I have a singular purpose and a calling. But actually I'm happiest when I'm doing lots of things. And I have to reconcile that."

IN FRONT OF THE CAMERA

"The blessing and curse of my life is that I think I thrive when I have a singular purpose and a calling. But actually I'm happiest when I'm doing lots of things. And I have to reconcile that."

Greta posing for a photo during a promotional run for the 2008 film *Baghead*.

IN FRONT OF THE CAMERA

Greta and Ben Stiller in a frame from the 2010 movie *Greenberg*.

NOAH'S (STORY) ARC

A break came in 2010. After appearing in *Yeast* in 2008 with the Safdie brothers and horror icon Ti West's early thriller *The House of The Devil* in 2009, Greta was cast in Noah Baumbach's *Greenberg* opposite Ben Stiller. Noah had seen Greta in *Hannah Takes the Stairs* and mentioned the actress to his agent, who signed her. When it came time to cast *Greenberg*, Greta again came up in conversation.

Working on *Greenberg* was a total one-eighty from the lo-fi world she had previously been involved in—there were auditions and trailers and a big-name cast and a real script. "In many ways, I felt like this was my first film," she told the *New York Times*.

Greta's discerning mom was also pleased with the new direction. "My mom said that people were starting to think that I'm really inarticulate," Greta joked with *New York Magazine*. "And I was like, 'Mom! Who speaks in full sentences anyway?' Well, Barack Obama, maybe. You can hear that man's commas. But I'm not giving speeches." Christine Gerwig also invested in cable TV for the first time ever, "so she can watch E!" Greta told the *New York Times*.

Greta and Noah's serendipitous connection was the meta meet-cute that spawned a new era in both of their careers. As *Collider* has hailed, "They make each other better... *Greenberg* is both literally and sub-textually a film about an artist falling in love with Gerwig... it felt like Baumbach was curating his entire style around the new burst of energy at the center of his film."

Greta with Rhys Ifans and Ben Stiller in a restaurant scene from the 2010 movie *Greenberg*.

Having Words with Noah Baumbach

Finding the right creative partner is sometimes even more difficult than finding the perfect match in a life partner. Egos can easily become involved and just as easily bruised, opinions about direction can cause huge rifts, and the work is incredibly precious to both sides. However, Greta and Noah have that once-in-a-lifetime kind of chemistry that has always allowed them to work well together and deliver award-winning material.

"Working together isn't hard. It's very easy," Greta admitted to the *Guardian*. "You find people you collaborate well with, but you don't want to be too precious about it. It's like a band. Except, with bands, everyone ends up hating each other. I think we trust that it'll ebb and flow."

So, how does it all get to the page? As Greta once described the setup to *Time Out,* she and Noah had separate writing corners in their New York home, where the work was done. They each took sections to own, crafting the passages individually, and then came together to share ideas in a workshop setting.

"We don't write in the same room together at a keyboard. It's more like we'll gather," she explained. "There'll be some raw material to start with of pages that don't necessarily fit in a story, and then we'll read them out loud and then talk about what the story is, what the world is, what the characters are, and then we'll each go away and generate more pages, trade, read them out loud again, talk through it more, and then at a certain point where the thing starts taking shape, we'll start saying, 'I can't crack this scene. Can you have a go at it?'"

GRETA

Greta and Noah Baumbach having a laugh on the red carpet at the UK premiere of *White Noise* in London, October 2022.

Some of their dialogue is culled from real-life conversations between the pair. In *Greenberg*, for example, Florence speaks a part about being way past her college expiration date and wondering if anyone cares if she wakes up each day, which is an off-the-cuff statement Greta made to Noah, one of the first times they met. They also have a pact that the script needs to be performed with 100% accuracy by actors, "right down to any extra 'likes' and 'you knows'" (the *Guardian*).

"Writing's always hard no matter what," Greta told *Gentlewoman UK*, "but I think we've both been aware that with the ones we do together there becomes a kind of third voice, where our voices intersect and meld and create this other thing that neither of us could do on our own."

IN FRONT OF THE CAMERA

"I think we've both been aware that with the ones we do together there becomes a kind of third voice, where our voices intersect and meld and create this other thing that neither of us could do on our own."

Greta with Noah Baumbach at the 92nd Annual Academy Awards in Los Angeles, California, February 2020.

Before meeting Greta, Noah was already known for his own works like 2005's *The Squid and the Whale*, 2007's *Margot at the Wedding*, and a few titles he co-wrote with Wes Anderson. But he too has echoed the sentiment about Greta bettering his work, telling *Vogue*, "Since we've been together, the work I've done, even that hasn't technically involved her, is hugely influenced by her. I think I could get in my head too much in my earlier career. She's helped me lose myself."

While Noah and Greta's dynamic has made some believe their working relationship is that of a master and his muse, Greta would like to have a word about that. "I remember being very frustrated by that and wanting to correct it," she told *Vogue*. While Noah has no doubt become a hugely important collaborator in her career, they are very much equal influences that feed off each other, with each presenting a similar naturalistic, deep, insightful, and charming style to their movies, particularly in the snappy dialogue and centralism around families. "I don't mean to sound annoying, but I would have done it anyway," she clapped back at a *Guardian* journalist when he prodded the actress/director on Noah helping her find her voice in film. "I will find that one door and then push it wide open. I'm lucky to find collaborators and kindred spirits. But I don't need a man, and I would have done it anyway."

For *Greenberg*, Greta was in a cast with Noah's then-wife, actress Jennifer Jason Leigh (who co-wrote the script with Noah). To get into character to play personal assistant Florence Marr, Greta actually tagged around with Jennifer's mother, screenwriter Barbara Turner, for a month. As Florence, Greta plays the sweet, affable foil to Ben Stiller's morose Roger Greenberg, who has just had a nervous breakdown and is down on his luck after mucking up his once promising rock-star life.

Greta's work in the film was largely applauded: the *New Yorker* said she was "lovely here, in her first big mainstream role," while lauded critic Roger Ebert said, "I have a weakness for actresses like Greta Gerwig. She looks reasonable and approachable. Some actresses are all edges and polish. This one, you could look up and see her walking

IN FRONT OF THE CAMERA

"I will find that one door and then push it wide open. I'm lucky to find collaborators and kindred spirits. But I don't need a man, and I would have done it anyway."

Greta with Ben Stiller and Noah Baumbach promoting *Greenberg* at the 60th Annual Berlin International Film Festival in Germany, February 2010.

dreamily through a bookstore, possibly with a Penguin Classic already in her hand." Many others pointed out the positive glow and refreshing disposition she brought to the thematically dour film. It's a reputation that would carry into future projects, with Greta's natural kindness, relatable and down-to-earth persona seeping into her characters. "People are like, 'You're always happy and you always seem high!'" Greta jokingly told the *New York Post*. "I don't want to be the girl everyone thinks is high!"

Greenberg established Greta in larger and respected Hollywood circles. But it also established the close professional *and* personal bond between her and Noah. The couple—who are said to have become romantically involved in 2011 or 2012, after Noah and ex-wife Jennifer Jason Leigh split in 2010—have worked on four additional films together, to date, including 2013's *Frances Ha*, 2015's *Mistress America*, and of course, 2023's *Barbie*. They also teamed up on 2022's

IN FRONT OF THE CAMERA

Greta with Adam Driver, Noah Baumbach, Don Cheadle, and Jodie Turner-Smith during the premiere of *White Noise* at the 79th Annual Venice International Film Festival in Italy, August 2022.

Opposite: Greta posing on the red carpet at the UK premiere of *White Noise* in London, October 2022.

White Noise, an adaptation of Don DeLillo's breakout novel, though Noah wrote the script solo while Greta took on the role of leading lady Babette. They are also parents to two young sons, Harold (born in 2019, right around the time of *Little Women*) and his younger brother, Isadore, born in 2023, right around the time of *Barbie*. Greta is also a stepmother to Noah's teenage son Rohmer from his previous relationship. After more than a decade together, Greta and Noah tied the knot in December 2023.

But before marriage and children, Noah and Greta's "babies" were their film collaborations. *Frances Ha* was a true standout. Shot in black-and-white in homage to French new wave cinema, it follows its titular character, Frances Halladay, a struggling dancer played by Greta, as she vagabonds her way around New York, Paris, and back home to Sacramento while she tries to figure out her unraveling friendships and her life—and how to support herself. Greta at first scoffed at the idea

of playing a role she wrote. As she told the *Guardian*, "It feels kind of disgusting, like baking a cake and eating it yourself. Like, I wrote it, and now I'm doing it! It felt very Orson Welles."

Even so, the then-actress earned stellar reviews for her part, with the *Independent* declaring, "Gerwig superbly incarnates the contradictions of this insecure woman." The *Village Voice* proclaimed, "No other movie has allowed [Greta] to display her colors like this." And the *Guardian* shared that Greta "dominates the movie" in a "wonderful performance that never becomes ingratiating." Here, too, Greta's script choices revolve around the worlds she knows—Frances grew up in Sacramento, and when she goes home for the holidays to visit family and high school friends, her parents are played by none other than Gordon and Christine Gerwig. The role earned Greta her first award nominations, including one for a Best Actress—Comedy or Musical Golden Globe.

Greta with Lola Kirke in a still from 2015's *Mistress America*.

"I still can't believe it. I keep thinking someone is going to call and say they made a mistake. I'm so honored," she shared with *Entertainment Weekly* upon learning of her inclusion in the category alongside Julie Delpy, Julia Louis-Dreyfus, Meryl Streep, and Amy Adams, who ended up winning. "All the women in the category are so amazing. I'm overwhelmed . . . I'm so honored and completely overwhelmed . . . I'm just very happy right now. I can't make sense!"

For 2015's *Mistress America*, Greta again teamed with Noah to write the script, and she played an essential character. Like *Frances Ha* and many of Greta's solo works to come, *Mistress America* revolves around the deep layers of female friendships and sisterhood and has Greta's ideology (with a side of humor) all over it. Greta plays Brooke Cardinas, a Manhattaner nearing thirty, playing a great game of "fake it 'til you make it" until her eighteen-year-old would-be stepsister, Tracy (played by Lola Kirke), comes into the picture. Much of how Brooke responds

Greta as the complicated Brooke Cardinas in 2015's *Mistress America*.

Greta with Lucy Owen, Scott Shepher, Jason Butler Harner, Cara Seymour, and Max Baker after a performance of the play *The Village Bike* staged at the Lucille Lortel Theatre in New York, June 2014.

Greta with Carrie MacLemore and Megalyn Echikunwoke in a still from the 2011 movie *Damsels in Distress*.

Opposite: A portrait of Greta and Hamish Linklater taken at the Tribeca Film Festival during the world premiere of *Lola Versus* in New York, 2012.

IN FRONT OF THE CAMERA

"One of the things that happens when you write characters—and maybe this is my own sentimentality—is that I always find I have an instinct to protect them. Maybe as I age—every birthday—I'll get harder on them. I do think that your character is your fate and you can't avoid that. But I want to soften the impact and give some grace to the downfall. Otherwise, it's unbearable."

and reacts in the film came directly from Greta, who often butted heads with Noah about the direction, but she stayed strong in her convictions, which she has chalked up to being "very protective" of her characters she creates and owns, especially the women.

"One of the things that happens when you write characters—and maybe this is my own sentimentality—is that I always find I have an instinct to protect them," she told the *Guardian*. "Maybe as I age—every birthday–I'll get harder on them. I do think that your character is your fate and you can't avoid that. But I want to soften the impact and give some grace to the downfall. Otherwise, it's unbearable."

Of course, Greta appeared as an actress in *other* people's movies during this essential decade too. Among her healthy list of credits are more mainstream roles in the Ashton Kutcher–Natalie Portman rom-com *No Strings Attached* and Russell Brand's remake of *Arthur*, both in 2011. "I don't care if people don't like those movies. Those movies saved my fucking life," she told the *Hollywood Reporter*, sharing that she was doing anything to get hired post *Greenberg*.

Greta with Megalyn Echikunwoke, Carrie MacLemore, and Lio Tipton in a still from 2011 movie *Damsels in Distress*.

Another 2011 film, *Damsels in Distress*, returned her to more indie fair. Greta played Violet, who leads a trio of women standing up to the patriarchal environment on their college campus. Then in 2012 came *Lola Versus* and Woody Allen's *To Rome With Love*, though she has since disavowed working with the scandal-ridden director. (As she told the *New York Times* in early 2018, "If I had known then what I know now, I would not have acted in the film. I have not worked for him again, and I will not work for him again.")

In 2016, there was a part playing a free-spirited photographer in Mike Mills' acclaimed *20th Century Women* (for which she nabbed a Critics Choice Award nomination) and Pablo Larraín's Jackie Kennedy Onassis biopic *Jackie*, in which Greta took on the role of JFK-era White

IN FRONT OF THE CAMERA

House Social Secretary and the former first lady's friend and secretary Nancy Tuckerman. There were also parts on TV shows like *Portlandia* and *The Mindy Project*, in 2015 and 2016, respectively. And in 2014, Greta was tapped to star in and help write a *How I Met Your Mother* spin-off called *How I Met Your Dad*. The pilot didn't fare well in test markets and CBS pulled the plug on the show, but it was revived several years later as *How I Met Your Father*, starring Hilary Duff.

Before *How I Met Your Dad*, Greta and Noah also had another project in the works for HBO, a series based on Jonathan Franzen's book *The Corrections*, though that too was dropped by the network. A high point though came when Greta made her Broadway debut in this era, in a 2014 production of Penelope Skinner's *The Village Bike*,

Greta with Ethan Hawke in the 2015 film *Maggie Plan*.

Following: Greta taking the photographers' attention on the red carpet at the 70th Annual Cannes Film Festival in France, May 2017.

fulfilling a lifelong dream for the theater lover. During the show's month-long run, Greta was applauded for her acting, and she was later nominated for Best Actress in the Outer Critics Circle Awards.

WARMING UP THE DIRECTOR'S SEAT

By 2015, as Greta's acting journey was winding down and shortly before working on *Lady Bird*, things were starting to shift. What thrilled Greta at that point was making her own films. "It was big and scary, but it's also the thing that comes most naturally to me," she told *Vogue*.

With a decade of experience in front of the camera, Greta called her long tenure as an actress "my version of my 10,000 hours" (per the *New York Times*), the concept put forth by Malcolm Gladwell that it takes that long to master any craft. Surely critics had thought so too. The *New Yorker*'s Richard Brody had gone so far as to say Greta was "the most important new actor" to come around in those ten years, and the *New York Times* critic A. O. Scott hailed Greta as "the definitive screen actress of her generation." *Los Angeles Times* called her more of the "accidental *it* girl."

Greta was lauded for playing oddball, imperfect characters with precision and a relatability factor that was hard to deny. She seemed like a real human on screen and not like she was portraying someone. As *New York Magazine* described her roles, Greta became the "sweetheart of a certain early adult angst." People could see themselves in her and learned through her. By 2016, Greta's acting prowess got her an invitation to be a member of the Academy of Motion Picture Arts and Sciences in the Actors Branch.

But Greta wanted something more for herself and her career. "I started making films in 2006. It's 2016. That's a pretty good run, and I feel like I have not settled, which is a nice thing. And I don't feel like the mountain is behind me, which is also a nice thing," she told the *Hollywood Reporter* at the time, adding, "One of the hard, hard things about acting [is] you're not kept warm at night by the things you used to do."

"Something that used to really hurt me is, people would say, 'Did you help write the script?' And I'd say: 'I co-wrote it. I didn't *help* to write it.' It used to make my blood rise."

There were other developments in her acting career that weren't sitting well with the talent. Chief among them was the fact that some assumed she was relegated to appearing on the screen and diminished her other important movie role—helping to shape the films she was in. "Something that used to really hurt me is, people would say, 'Did you help write the script?' And I'd say: 'I co-wrote it. I didn't *help* to write it,'" she told the *New York Times*. "It used to make my blood rise."

By the time she was working on French film *Eden* with writer-director Mia Hansen-Løve in 2014 and *Maggie's Plan* with writer-director Rebecca Miller in 2015, Greta had already been working steadfastly on her own solo material. She finished the *Lady Bird* script in 2015, and she finally had the mentorship and example she needed to push forward on her own.

Greta in the 2011 film *Arthur*.

Opposite: Greta with Adam Brody, Analeigh Tipton, and Whit Stillman at the 68th Venice Film Festival in Venice, Italy, September 2011.

IN FRONT OF THE CAMERA 103

"It's no accident that I worked with [Rebecca] and turned around and made my film," Greta said, per *Indie Wire*. "I already had a draft by then. Being with her gave me confidence." Regarding working with Mia, Greta told the *New York Times*, "She said that the other young male writers there treated her dismissively because they thought of her as [filmmaker] Olivier [Assayas'] girlfriend, who got there because she was his girlfriend, and how they changed when she had her first movie at Cannes, when she was in her twenties. All of a sudden they looked at her like they'd never seen her before. I hung onto that story. All those little pieces I put in my pocket. I think I needed these little signs."

And even though she initially conceived of *Lady Bird* as a script she'd complete for someone else to bring to the screen, those pivotal run-ins with other female moviemakers gave Greta the impetus she needed to direct it herself—even if she had no real experience doing so. "I thought, Yes, there is more to learn, but you are not going to keep learning it by not doing it," she told *New York Times*. "You will only now learn the next part if you go ahead and do it."

Plus, the great Francis Ford Coppola reminded her she wouldn't be the first actor to make the jump, as Greta recalled to *Vogue*. "[He] said to me that all the best directors had been actors. He said, 'I acted. Marty [Scorsese] acted and Steven [Spielberg] acted. Orson [Welles] acted.' I was like, 'Well, what a wonderful group!'"

"I thought, Yes, there is more to learn, but you are not going to keep learning it by not doing it. You will only now learn the next part if you go ahead and do it."

Greta's World
Frances Halladay

Before Greta was covering the highs and lows of teenagehood in *Lady Bird* and *Little Women,* she was navigating the tricky course of quarter-life crises in *Frances Ha.* It was a similarly precious time of incredible transition, when *real* adulthood starts to set in, you have to figure out who your friends are, how you're going to pay the bills, and how to make passion projects successful or let them fall to the wayside.

When the movie came out in 2013, Greta was on the cusp of turning thirty herself and felt incredibly close to the material she was writing with Noah, often advocating for the impulses and actions of Frances because, well, who could possibly know better?

Frances, like *Lady Bird,* shares characteristics that mirror Greta's own life—she's a dancer, she was born and raised in Sacramento, and, hell, even Greta's real-life parents (Gordon and Christine) make cameos as Frances' own family. It was this realism that Greta brought to the film, making it hard to tell where the line was drawn between fiction and fact, giving her character extra dimension. It's no coincidence Greta's take on Frances hoisted her further into Hollywood's elite and earned her that first Golden Globe nomination—she made Frances incredibly believable because the character was etched from real-life experience.

Greta in a still frame from the 2013 film *Frances Ha.*

IN FRONT OF THE CAMERA

"I think for me, the period of life right after college, there's kind of a grace period where being a mess is charming and interesting. And then I think when you hit around 27, it stops being charming and interesting, and it starts being kind of pathological," she told NPR. "I think that anybody who does anything in the arts feels very close to failure, because it seems like it's so possible to not be doing it, because even when things are going well, it feels like they're always about to fall apart and about to not work . . . [Frances is] in an emotional place where I think I definitely went through, where she's realizing her friends aren't her family, which is difficult."

Seeing these raw breakdowns and breakthroughs on screen isn't exactly the material of the typical "happy ending" paradigm, which makes characters like Frances Ha so compelling, if not also brave. As *Time Out* says, "They're the unglamorous tales of women who are losing, set in a time when the egocentrics on social media show everyone as winning."

Greta dancing in a scene from 2013 film *Frances Ha*.

Greta ruminating in a bathtub in a still from 2013 film *Frances Ha*.

Greta arriving at a special screening of *Frances Ha* held at the Vista Theatre in Los Angeles, California, May 2013.

Following: A still of Greta in *Lola Versus* in 2012.

IN FRONT OF THE CAMERA 109

"I think that anybody who does anything in the arts feels very close to failure, because it seems like it's so possible to not be doing it, because even when things are going well, it feels like they're always about to fall apart and about to not work."

The Holy Film Trifecta

Take 4

> "I want to produce women's films, because I think women want to see films made by people who know what they're talking about, what the experience is."
>
> —Greta speaking at the 2017 Women in Entertainment Summit

Greta Gerwig was certainly not the first woman filmmaker to make a name for herself on the big screen. Before she entered the conversation with her remarkable debut *Lady Bird*, there was Jane Campion, Ava DuVernay, Patty Jenkins, Nancy Meyers, Nora Ephron, Amy Heckerling, Sofia Coppola, and Kathryn Bigelow, among others, who

---

Greta with her pretty in pink *Barbie* cast on the set of the 2023 movie.

also gained recognition for their work. Yet the short list is still quite a *short* list, with female directors often having their achievements weighed against what male directors have been able to accomplish in the same field. "You just look forward to the day when it doesn't mean anything," Greta once told *Time* about the role of gender in filmmaking and carrying the loaded title of *woman* director.

Yet Greta has been hugely impactful in bringing Hollywood to task, demanding more representation and more perspectives in film—and, at the same time, inspiring other women moviemakers to believe there is a future for them. To understand the impression Greta Gerwig has made not only on modern filmmaking, but also as a heroine of the modern feminist, "too-much girl" power movement (*Dazed*), one only needs to look at the incredible things she's been able to accomplish as a writer and director in such a short amount of time—not even enough years to count on two hands.

Greta is the only director in filmmaking history to have her first three solo feature films (*Lady Bird*, *Little Women*, and *Barbie*) nominated for Best Picture by the Academy Awards. She's also the only solo female director to surpass the $1 billion gross threshold. Talk about totally smashing the glass ceiling and putting together the pieces to create a pathway for other women to follow.

"My desire to direct and my determination to direct was a feeling of, 'I've been given all these gifts, and I know all those women, and I know all those professors and all the women who came before me.' And it's not good enough if I don't do it," Greta told *Bust* shortly after the release of *Lady Bird*. "I'm letting them down and I'm letting the next generation of those women down because—I felt like there was a sense of the gauntlet being thrown down to all of us."

Oscar nominee for Best Director and Original Screenplay for *Lady Bird,* Greta arriving on the red carpet of Oscars in Hollywood, 2018.

GRETA

Greta's Rave Reviews

Since her mainstream breakthrough in the 2010 film *Greenberg*, Greta has become nothing short of a critical darling. In copious reviews in both blogs and high-brow arts bibles, many have been drawn into Greta's orbit, singing her praises as both an actor and a director. Here's just a sample of what critics have had to say over the past fifteen years.

"What Ms. Gerwig does in 'Greenberg' confirms a suspicion that began to bubble up through the diffidence and indirection of movies like 'Hannah Takes the Stairs,' 'LOL' and 'Nights and Weekends,' . . . Ms. Gerwig. . . may well be the definitive screen actress of her generation . . . She seems to be embarked on a project, however piecemeal and modestly scaled, of redefining just what it is we talk about when we talk about acting." —*New York Times'* review of *Greenberg*

"Gerwig may be famed for acting like a non-actor, but she's an extraordinarily accomplished actor (as she proved in 'Damsels in Distress'), and here she puts the movie on her back and carries it from beginning to end . . . The "arrangements" (in this case, the script and its directorial adornments), put her in front, as a soloist." —*The New Yorker*'s review of *Frances Ha*

"In addition to quippy, smart dialogue, Lola is memorable because she's played by bundle-of-contradictions actress Greta Gerwig . . . Gerwig is daffy but smart, she manages to seem confident and confused at the same moment and she always seems to be puzzled by her own gawky physicality. . . All of which means Gerwig is usually fascinating, even if the movie around her is not." —*Pioneer Press'* review of *Lola Versus*

"Greta Gerwig's *Lady Bird* is big-screen perfection . . . What Ms. Gerwig has done—and it's by no means a small accomplishment—is to infuse one of the most convention-bound, rose-colored genres in American cinema with freshness and surprise . . . The script is exceptionally well-written, full of wordplay and lively argument." —*New York Times'* review of *Lady Bird*

"A cozy, polished and masterly cinematic rendering of Louisa May Alcott's immortal 19th-century novel . . . *Little Women* solidifies Gerwig's one-of-a-kind voice on the page and behind the camera, opening up the classic in a blissful and innovative screen adaptation that feels ageless and vastly of today." —*RogerEbert.com's* review of *Little Women*

"*Barbie* is Gerwig's best film to date. It is a coalescence of themes from her entire body of work, from the exploration of the dynamics between men and women to the desire for women to define themselves as individuals . . . Barbie herself goes through a journey of not just becoming human, but learning what that means, particularly becoming a woman in the real world. The ending sequence . . . celebrates what Gerwig's films strive to capture: life in its fullest form." —*Screen Rant's* review of *Barbie*

"My desire to direct and my determination to direct was a feeling of, 'I've been given all these gifts, and I know all those women, and I know all those professors and all the women who came before me.' And it's not good enough if I don't do it. I'm letting them down and I'm letting the next generation of those women down because – I felt like there was a sense of the gauntlet being thrown down to all of us."

Saoirse Ronan and Lucas Hedges in a still from the 2017 film *Lady Bird*.

Greta behind the camera while filming 2017's Lady Bird.

LUCK BE A *LADY BIRD*

Whether or not there was a sense of pressure, there was an incredible sense of duty with Greta's first film—and it turned into a monumental undertaking. The script for *Lady Bird* was originally 350 pages long (the equivalent of a six-hour movie). "That's my way. I go too big and then I find the essence and pare it back," she told *Screen Daily*. The original had a lot of narrative loops that, even to her, made it feel disjointed. After many, *many* drafts, Greta was able to scale the script back to about 90 pages after figuring out the core of the story, which was *Mothers and Daughters*. That, in fact, was the original name of the film.

Greta had great interest in zeroing in on that particular "rich relationship" like another filmmaker might have in guy-and-girl dynamics. As the new director told NPR's Terry Gross, "I don't know any woman who has a simple relationship with their mother or with their daughter. I feel that it's not something that's given as much cinematic time as it is worthy of it, so I wanted to give it a space that you would usually reserve for a romantic relationship . . . it kind of follows these ups and downs and these fights, and also these moments of real connection."

The other major theme of *Lady Bird* is the coming-of-age tale of a complex, not-a-girl-not-yet-a-woman character. The opportunity to make the film came along at the perfect time in Greta's own life, as Lady Bird's journey paralleled how she was growing in her own career field. But the spin she put on the narrative was markedly different from the established mores. For decades, a large part of our collective knowledge of adolescent tales has come from watching boys becoming men—*Lord of The Flies*, *The Outsiders*, *Stand By Me*, literally *Boy* and *Boyhood*. In homing in on the tale of Christine "Lady Bird" McPherson, Greta gives us the other side of the coin.

"I don't know any woman who has a simple relationship with their mother or with their daughter. I feel that it's not something that's given as much cinematic time as it is worthy of it, so I wanted to give it a space that you would usually reserve for a romantic relationship."

Greta in an Immaculate Heart hoodie while on the set of the 2017 film *Lady Bird*.

Greta taking a moment with actors Lucas Hedges and Saoirse Ronan on the set of the 2017 film *Lady Bird*.

Following: Saoirse Ronan and Lucas Hedges walking hand in hand on the set of the 2017 film *Lady Bird*.

"What is *Boyhood,* but for a girl? What is *The 400 Blows,* but for **a girl**? What is **personhood** for young women?"

"What is *Boyhood*, but for a girl? What is *The 400 Blows*, but for a girl? What is personhood for young women?" she pondered to the *New York Times*, narrowing in on her unique perspective for *Lady Bird*. The article astutely adds that, "in most films, girls exist to be looked at. Sometimes they help a male protagonist come to a realization about himself. Sometimes they die. Gerwig makes Lady Bird the one who looks: at boys but also houses, magazines, books, clothes, and at the city of Sacramento." For viewers, seeing life through Lady Bird's eyes was the equivalent of a 3D movie without the stupid glasses.

With a final script in hand, Greta knew—much like she did with *Barbie*—that she was the only person capable of directing *Lady Bird* in order to see its vision all the way through, even if she had little experience in the director's chair. "I've always wanted to direct," she told *Dazed*, and there was no time like the present to pull the trigger. As she figured, being thrown into the lion's den was going to give her a lot more knowledge than studying the craft from afar. "I've learned about as much as I'm going to learn by sitting on the sidelines and I certainly have a lot more to learn but it's going to be by doing it—not by not doing it."

With the decision made, Greta then faced the huge task of finding someone to finance and produce the film, which meant pitching her idea to the men who fill the majority of the pool in Hollywood. And when she did, something interesting happened. "What I typically found was that if they had daughters or had been raised with sisters, they understood what it was, and if they didn't, they kind of couldn't believe that women actually fought like that, which was an interesting window into why some stories can't get told," she told the *New York Times*. "People don't understand that they're even a story to tell."

Eventually the person who did finance the project was Scott Rudin, a long-time collaborator of Noah Baumbach who had also worked with Greta on *Frances Ha* and *Mistress America*. She was hesitant at first to involve Scott, but once he got word of her project, he made the first move, asking if he could read it. "And in about twelve hours, he said he

"I've learned about as much as I'm going to learn by sitting on the sidelines and I certainly have a lot more to learn but it's going to be by doing it – not by not doing it."

Saoirse Ronan in deep thought in a still frame from the 2017 film *Lady Bird*.

THE HOLY FILM TRIFECTA

would produce it. It was a tremendously productive, wonderful working relationship," Greta shared with *Screen Daily*.

It's said that Greta had envisioned her dream cast early on, leaning into theater greats she respected like Tracy Letts and Laurie Metcalf to play Lady Bird's parents. Laurie Metcalf, who notably played Aunt Jackie in *Roseanne* (a show Greta didn't even see until *Lady Bird* wrapped), needed little prodding, telling Greta, "Currently I have a seventeen-year-old child that's trying to kill me. So, I think this is exactly what I need to be doing right now" (*NoFilmSchool.com*).

Greta also had visions of Saoirse Ronan (who by then had already received Academy Award nominations for her roles in *Atonement* and *Brooklyn*) as the title character. The two first met at the Toronto International Film Festival in 2015, when Saoirse was promoting *Brooklyn* and Greta was in attendance for *Maggie's Plan*. After meeting, Greta simply gave her wished-upon leading lady the script for *Lady Bird*, without much added context, for her consideration. In doing so, without any superfluous disclaimers, Greta believed the actor could feel as close to experiencing the movie with its full integrity as possible. Because for Greta, always, "the writing [has] to be the thing that sells the script" (*Screen Daily*).

The method was also practical, as it introduced the proposed talent to the very staunch commitment Greta holds to always stick to the script. Unlike her foundational mumblecore days, when ad-libbing was encouraged to offer a natural dialogue, Greta told *Dazed*, "I don't do any improvisation on set . . . The process I've always had as a writer [is that] the script is the reason for making the film." It may come from her early love of theater, she rationalized with *Screen Daily*, "where the playwright is king. You don't change those words, you figure out how to make them work. You work for them, they don't work for you."

The trademark is a style choice she's classified as "word perfect," telling *60 Minutes*, "even if somebody swaps a word out, it doesn't sound right." Going line by line with a fine-tooth comb while on set has been a non-negotiable for Greta since the start and has continued

"I don't do any **improvisation** on set . . . The process I've always had as a **writer** [is that] the **script** is the reason for making the **film**."

as recently as *Barbie*. The other filmmaking standard that Greta holds to is that she does not allow playback on her sets. "I hate when people need to watch playbacks immediately after watching the performance the actors just gave seconds before," she said in *Interview*.

Greta was so confident that Saoirse was the right pick for *Lady Bird* that she actually delayed filming for a half-year while the actress appeared in *The Crucible* on Broadway. While Saoirse completed the run, from March to June of 2016, there were bonding sessions to fill the time and get the cast acquainted with each other. Greta brought them all, including Timothée Chalamet, Beanie Feldstein, and Lucas Hedges, on trips to New York to simply hang out. The quality time continued in Los Angeles when production on the film finally kicked off in the summer of 2016, as Greta chose to hold rehearsals in the carefree environment of her rental apartment, concluding each session with a no-holds-barred dance party.

"I wanted them to feel connected . . . We would also do things like have dance parties because it's a really good way to get to know each other and I wanted everyone to feel loose and free," she told *Screen Daily*. As she added in an *Interview* conversation with Francis Ford Coppola, "I wanted there to be this core of love and understanding with each other that we could work from. It needed to feel like a communal experience, not an individual one."

That sense of camaraderie, security, and work hard/play hard balance has become the real ethos of a Greta Gerwig set. She routinely hosts experiential opportunities for her casts, like the prom she threw for everyone involved with *Lady Bird*, taking her *Little Women* actors to visit Louisa May Alcott's grave, and also pressing the *Little Women* cast to choose a poem to recite to their castmates as an icebreaker. Most recently, she invited all the Barbies to a hotel sleepover; Kens were welcome to hang, too, but, naturally, weren't allowed to spend the night. Greta also encourages families to come along on shooting days to provide a communal and loving environment where everyone feels safe to get into character. Call it her maternal instinct—she's always been mama bear, incredibly protective not only of her characters but also the real-life humans playing them. "If you're an asshole on a Greta Gerwig set, there's no hope for you," Ken actor Simu Liu told *Elle*.

There have been so many fun quirks in Greta's approach as a filmmaker that you can start to understand why so many actors and actresses return to working with her time and again: Saoirse Ronan, Timothée Chalamet, and Tracy Letts have all signed on for multiple roles in Greta's films, and Saoirse and Margot Robbie have gone on record to say that Greta's directorial style has inspired them to want to one day pursue the field too.

Beanie Feldstein and Saoirse Ronan in an emotional scene from the 2017 film *Lady Bird*.

THE HOLY FILM TRIFECTA

Creating With Adult ADHD

In her 2023 interview with the *Guardian*, Greta opened up to the journalist about her diagnosis of adult ADHD (attention-deficit/hyperactivity disorder) and the clarity it provided regarding her way of being and creating. According to the Mayo Clinic, ADHD can manifest as "difficulty paying attention, hyperactivity, and impulsive behavior."

Remarking in the article on how she had a "ton of energy at school" as a child, Greta added, "My mom was like, 'Let's sign her up for every activity. Let's tire her out.'"

As Greta has talked about at length, her interests have always been incredibly varied, from ballet to fencing to theater to acting to directing. "I've always had a tremendous amount of enthusiasm. I was just interested in, like, everything," she added in her *Guardian* chat. "I had a really active imagination. I had a lot of really deep feelings. I was emotional."

Greta making her *Lady Bird* cast laugh on the set of the 2017 film.

THE HOLY FILM TRIFECTA

Rather than a great, invisible Oz pulling the strings, Greta is incredibly hands-on and approachable, plus she has the same anxieties an actor does. She is someone who has Enya as her ringtone (to provide a sense of calm), who walks for miles when she gets writers block, and who once wore pairs of shoes gifted by fellow directors Miranda July and Rebecca Miller on the *Lady Bird* set any time she "needed a boost," per the *New York Times*. "It felt like, if you're looking for a sign, there you go!" said Greta.

Whatever the magic was in her directorial algorithm, it paid off. When *Lady Bird* was released in November 2017 by A24, shortly after premiering at the Telluride Film Festival, it landed in theaters with a perfect 10. "In the decade since her mumblecore origins, Greta Gerwig has found her voice, applying that unselfconscious honesty to her directorial debut," *Variety* hailed of Greta's "modest, miraculous low-budget gem that takes on a life of its own." *Time* declared it "the arrival of a bright new voice" in the director pool, while the *New Yorker* praised the film for its "exquisite dialogue," and said of Greta, "if there's any justice in the industry, Gerwig is launched" as a director.

Lady Bird was also added to "best of the year" lists by *Time*, the National Board of Review, and the American Film Institute. In the *Time's* 100 Most Influential People of the Year issue in 2018, Greta was included with an honorary piece written by Steven Spielberg who said, "Not every year does a filmmaker's solo feature debut sweep you up in its sweetness and pain, in its humility and frankness, and in its confidence in the art and craft of filmmaking . . . Greta has a kind of momentum that feels like it must help contain a million good ideas from flying out of the atmosphere. It's not a nervous energy; it's an engaged one."

Lady Bird not only raked in $79 million (a huge surplus over its $10 million budget), but it also had a 100% score on *Rotten Tomatoes* for months—until film critic Cole Smithey marked it down, believing the film shouldn't have a perfect grade. The horror of that one bad review caused an uproar on social media, marking the first but not last time

GRETA

Greta's titles have become viral topics of conversation. "Just woke up from my nap and lady bird is now at 99% on rotten tomatoes wtf did yall do," one person wrote on X. Currently, *Lady Bird* is rated 99 percent on the critical aggregate site—still a huge feat.

The film was also award show fodder. Saoirse, Laurie, and Greta were all nominated for Golden Globes in 2018 for Best Actress, Best Supporting Actress, and Best Screenplay, respectively, while the film

Amanda Seyfried giving Greta the award for Best Screenplay for *Lady Bird* at the 33rd Independent Spirit Awards in Santa Monica, California, March 2018.

THE HOLY FILM TRIFECTA 133

"I remember when Sofia Coppola was nominated and how much that meant to me. I remember when Kathryn Bigelow won and what that felt like, and I feel like those women are the reason I was able to do this."

GRETA

was up for Best Motion Picture—Musical or Comedy. At the Academy Awards the same year, the three women were all nominated in the same categories, with the film also nominated for Best Picture and Best Director (at the time, it was the fifth occasion *ever* that a woman was nominated in the best director category). Talk about a huge coup for a first-time filmmaker.

"I've been in various states of laughing and crying and yelling with joy," Greta told *Entertainment Weekly* at the time. "I remember when Sofia Coppola was nominated and how much that meant to me. I remember when Kathryn Bigelow won and what that felt like, and I feel like those women are the reason I was able to do this." Greta added, also thinking about those who may feel the same way about her, "I hope that they look at this and they think, 'I'm going to go make my movie.'"

Though none of the nominations turned into wins at the Academy Awards, Saoirse won her category at the Golden Globes and *Lady Bird* took home the Best Motion Picture—Musical or Comedy title the same night. When time came to accept the award, Greta was chosen to speak on behalf of the film. Among the many people she thanked, she included "my beautiful cast" and "the goddesses" Saoirse and Laurie, her parents, and "the people of Sacramento, who gave me roots and wings."

But one person she forgot to thank was her partner, Noah Baumbach. "I had an entire speech that I was going to give and I got up there and none of it came out . . . I looked at Oprah and I was like, 'It's gone,'" she told the ladies of *The View* during an appearance the day after the Golden Globes telecast. "I had a whole thing about him. He's my favorite writer and my favorite first reader . . . As I was coming back to the table, he was already looking at me and said, 'Please don't feel bad.'"

Greta in front of her *Lady Bird* cast accepting the award for Best Motion Picture—Musical or Comedy at the 75th Annual Golden Globe Awards in Beverly Hills, California, January 2018.

MATURING WITH *LITTLE WOMEN*

Noah and Greta's careers would lovingly come into the crosshairs again in the 2020 award season, as Greta's next film, *Little Women*, and Noah's compelling movie *Marriage Story* were nominated for six Academy Awards each, including going toe-to-toe in the Best Picture category (both ultimately lost to *Parasite*). Neither was included in the Best Director category, however; if they had been, they would've been the first couple to do so in moviemaking history. But, never say never.

In many ways, *Little Women* is also a coming-of-age story, Greta's go-to repertoire. The moviemaker has always been incredibly interested in times of transition and change, and the life experiences that come with them. Her movies feel like a guidebook for anyone going through those times, like a deep talk with a mother or older sister. Unlike *Lady Bird*, which is set post-Y2K, *Little Women* is a Civil War saga, yet both are told with Greta's precise aptitude for dialing into a universal perspective of what it means to grow up as a young woman in any era in America. As *Vogue* declares, "Gerwig [has] been anointed patron saint of a certain kind of ambling early adulthood . . . giving voice to the quotidian dramas that plague her and her kind, first as an actress, then as a writer, and finally as a director, for her entire career."

Greta told *Vanity Fair* that she'd had the concept for the movie adaptation of *Little Women* dancing in her head since she was about seven, "but I had no concept that my life would go in a direction that would allow me to make it into a real movie." She actually started working on a script in 2014, even before making *Lady Bird*, which makes one wonder how much her first original screenplay's themes may have been affected by the classic tale.

Little Women, written in 1868 by Louisa May Alcott, has seen a dozen or more adaptations over time, with seven major films/TV mini-series, including the 1994 iteration with Winona Ryder, Kirsten Dunst,

---

Top: Greta behind the camera while on the set of her 2019 film *Little Women*.

Bottom: Saoirse Ronan and Timothée Chalamet in a still from the 2019 film *Little Women*.

Claire Danes, and Susan Sarandon, also directed by a woman, Gillian Armstrong. But as the *Guardian* claims, "only one gave Jo [March] the ending she deserves." The article digs into Greta's "meta-twist" for the final scenes of her take on the story, in which she provides two concurrent happy endings—that Jo marries and has a family with the professor and that she still gets to have her career and see her book printed. It's a "nod to the end [Louisa] wanted to write," says the article, "and thanks to Gerwig, Jo finally exists in a time when women *can* have all that."

There's much to be said about Greta's own experiences influencing her writing, or at the least putting her in that existential headspace. In March 2019, nine months before *Little Women* came out, Greta became a first-time mother to son Harold Ralph Gerwig Baumbach. In fact, he was born twenty-four hours after she turned in her *Little Women* script, and Harold famously appeared with his mother on her big *Vogue* cover story the following January.

Greta talking with Meryl Streep on the set of the 2019 film *Little Women*.

"I was always scared about being a **mother**, in terms of what it would mean for what I was able to do . . . But I've just been very **moved** by **women** who've **claimed** all of it."

Greta directing Emma Watson on the set of the 2019 film *Little Women*.

"I was always scared about being a mother," she told *Vogue*, "in terms of what it would mean for what I was able to do . . . But I've just been very moved by women who've claimed all of it." Those examples of women who had it all were taken to heart as Greta welcomed her two babies around the same time as two of her biggest projects—Harold with *Little Women* and Isadore during the time of *Barbie*—always able to give both of her jobs her full attention. If she wasn't nursing while on set, she was bringing her children to studios with her. "I felt like he was being christened by Meryl [Streep]," she told *Vogue* about Harold spending a large amount of time around the acting legend. Lucky kid. When pressed by the magazine if there were any similarities between rearing children and films, Greta said, "Yes, I think that feeling of forever being underqualified and kind of awed by the thing."

When Greta heard through the Hollywood grapevine that Sony

Greta and Saoirse Ronan on set during the making of the 2019 film *Little Women*.

Pictures, with producers Amy Pascal, Robin Swicord, and Denise Di Novi, were intent on making a *Little Women* movie for a new generation (more than a two decades after Gillian Armstrong's version came out), she was hellbent on joining the project. Originally, according to *Indie Wire*, actress Sarah Polley was on tap to write it. But Greta told her agent, "I have to go talk to them. I have to write and direct this because I have an idea." She hadn't made *Lady Bird* at that point, but Sony liked what they heard. Originally, Greta was hired only to craft the script, but after the wild success of *Lady Bird*, talks picked up, and Greta was given the studio's blessing to fully helm *Little Women*.

But that also meant whittling down her script, as she had with *Lady Bird*. She again had copious amounts of material, this time amounting to approximately 400 pages. As Greta told *Vogue*, she sojourned to a cabin in Big Sur, California, to tackle the editing process: "I needed to

THE HOLY FILM TRIFECTA 141

spend some alone time with Louisa." She did so via extensive research, notably by pouring over Louisa's journals and the popular books at the time. The article goes on to detail how then-36-year-old Greta was the same age as Louisa May Alcott when she wrote *Little Women*, and was such a big believer in signs, she hired an astrologer to analyze the two writers' celestial charts, said Greta, "Because so much of making art requires some amount of mysticism."

The idea Greta pitched to Sony was twofold. First, she wanted to begin the film when the little women were adults, looking back at their lives in flashback scenes. "Because I was an adult. And because that was the part of the story that suddenly spoke to me in a way that had never really resonated before," she told *Vanity Fair*. In fact, Greta had serendipitously re-read *Little Women* in her early thirties, before she was even attached to the project. As she explained to NPR, "I was actually moving apartments . . . I hadn't read it for a long time, and so I opened it, and I found myself sucked back in. And also, I felt like I'd never read it before."

The second component was symbolically infusing the story of Louisa herself into the script, something that only a writer's writer like Greta could pull off. After all, Greta often infuses her own ghost into her original works. "[Louisa May Alcott] made the lives of girls and women a best-seller. That was extraordinary," she told *Vanity Fair*. She noted all the ways in which Louisa's life parallels Jo's, but also realized, "there's places where they diverge. Most notably that Jo March gets married and has children and stops writing by the end of *Little Women*. And Louisa May Alcott never got married, never had children, and kept writing and owned her own copyright and became one of the wealthiest self-made women in America. And that, I felt like there was a lot to explore there."

Saoirse was also determined to be a part of *Little Women*. "Saoirse told me she was going to play Jo. She knew I was working on it and she said, 'I know your goal, you're writing it. I know you're writing and I'm going to play Jo,'" Greta recalled to *Vanity Fair*. "It felt like a very Jo thing to do,

"It felt like a very Jo thing to do, to kind of claim her space . . . It felt very similar actually to my going into Sony and telling them that they should hire me to write and direct this film when I'd never written and directed a film before alone in my life. It felt like Jo-slash-Louisa was operating through both of us."

Saoirse Ronan as Jo March in a scene from the 2019 film *Little Women*.

THE HOLY FILM TRIFECTA

to kind of claim her space . . . It felt very similar actually to my going into Sony and telling them that they should hire me to write and direct this film when I'd never written and directed a film before alone in my life. It felt like Jo slash Louisa was operating through both of us."

In addition to Saoirse, Greta assembled an all-star cast of Emma Watson (who replaced original Meg March, Emma Stone), Florence Pugh, Eliza Scanlen, Laura Dern, Bob Odenkirk, Tracy Letts, Timothée Chalamet, Chris Cooper, and of course the incredible Meryl Streep who, Greta noted, was very influential in the final script, with her own feminist perspectives coming to the forefront.

"We talked about it a lot because the book had meant a great deal to her . . . And the conversations I had with Meryl informed the script," Greta told *Vanity Fair*. "Meryl said, 'The thing you have to make the audience understand is it's not just that women couldn't vote, which they couldn't. And it's not just that they couldn't have jobs, which they couldn't. It's that they did not own anything . . . So that's the stakes of who are you going to marry because it's [as] if you had no options. I just essentially took that almost verbatim and gave it to Florence [Pugh's character Amy].'"

Little Women was shot on location in Concord, Massachusetts, in a near replica of the Orchard House where Louisa May Alcott spent her time. Greta imbued experiential learning opportunities for her cast, including visiting the real Orchard House, seeing the desk where the novel came to life and Louisa's extensive book collection, and then going to her gravesite in Sleepy Hollow.

Shooting days were filled with the same air of focused fun that had filled the *Lady Bird* set. The cast had to learn to do Civil War-era waltzes in perfect measure, but it wasn't in a stuffy ballroom with

Top: Emma Watson, Florence Pugh, Saoirse Ronan, and Eliza Scanlen in character as the March sisters on the set of the 2019 film *Little Women*.

Bottom: Greta behind the camera while directing *Little Women*.

Following: Florence Pugh, Emma Watson, Saoirse Ronan, and Eliza Scanlen as the March sisters in a still from the 2019 film *Little Women*.

"If you strip away this pre-Victorian morality, what you have is ambitious, passionate, angry, sexual, interesting women who don't fit into the boxes the world has given them."

period-appropriate music. The choreographer, Monica Bill Barnes, played David Bowie and the Cure as the soundtrack to learn the fancy footwork. Emma Watson led daily meditation and yoga sessions before work got started. There was a feminine energy that was contagious and came across on the reel, too, according to Saoirse. "Having so many girls leading the way on set definitely changed the tone," she told *Vogue*. "We were all completely hyper with each other, and Greta is such a girl's girl herself, she really captured that energy."

Greta also did an interesting thing with the dialogue in the film, 80 percent of which was true to Louisa May Alcott's own writing. During two weeks of rehearsals, she refined how her characters would talk. "I am having [the cast] say the dialogue with such controlled chaos and choreographed cacophony that it comes across as having just been written by me, when in fact every word is either from the book or Alcott's journals, letters, or another book she's written," she told *Time*. "If you strip away this pre-Victorian morality, what you have is ambitious, passionate, angry, sexual, interesting women who don't fit into the boxes the world has given them."

Everything from the vintage costuming to the set design was also incredibly well thought-out. As Greta told the Associated Press, "I didn't want it to be beautiful at the expense of being real. But I did want it to feel like you wish you can jump inside and live in there We spent a lot of time building shot diagrams and, with the production designer, the costume designer, and my (director of photography), plotting out exactly how we were going to see everything and make it bursting with life."

Viewers and critics caught on to that thoughtfulness too. Upon its release on Christmas Day 2019, *Little Women* received rave reviews and smashed box office records. "Greta Gerwig refreshes a literary classic

Top: Greta with Emma Watson, Saoirse Ronan, and Florence Pugh looking over the script for the 2019 film *Little Women*.

Bottom: Greta surrounded by her *Little Women* cast, including Timothée Chalamet, Saoirse Ronan, Florence Pugh, Eliza Scanlen, Laura Dern, and Chris Cooper, in a promotional image for the 2019 movie.

THE HOLY FILM TRIFECTA 149

with the help of a dazzling cast," said the *New York Times*, calling the film "an absolute gift . . . that embraces its source material with eager enthusiasm rather than timid reverence." *Vox* said, "It's a genuinely extraordinary screenplay in that it feels like a work of criticism, in the very best way . . . it's reconsidered with a depth of humanity and understanding of the time in which the book was written, infusing it with new life." And *Time* hailed it a "pure pleasure to watch . . . both respectful and invigorating, it's [Greta's] own inscription to a new generation, a reimagining that reaches out to young people making their way in the world today even as it's true to the manner in which Alcott herself—a woman writer in a field ruled by men—had to push her way forward."

The film brought in $206 million worldwide, a $56 million profit for Sony, per *Deadline*, and it was a strong contender during the 2020 award season. In addition to Golden Globe nominations for Best Performance by an Actress in a Motion Picture—Drama for Saoirse and Best Original Score for Alexandre Desplat, *Little Women* nabbed six Academy Award nominations, including Best Picture, Best Adapted Screenplay, Best Original Score, Best Costume Design, Best Actress for Saoirse Ronan, and Best Supporting Actress for Florence Pugh. It took home just one award, however, for Best Costume Design for Jacqueline Durran. Most egregiously, Greta was left out of the Best Director category just two years after being included for *Lady Bird*.

The word "snub" first reared its head around Greta's achievements at this time; 2020 Oscar presenter Natalie Portman even went so far as to wear a cape threaded with the names of the female directors who have been left out of the award category over time and included Greta's name in her statement-making red carpet fashion. "I wanted to recognize the women who were not recognized for their incredible work this year in my subtle way," Natalie said during pre-telecast interviews. Of course, this would not be the first time this controversy would come up for Greta Gerwig.

Greta posing during a *Little Women* promotional run in London, England, December 2019.

THE *BARBIE* BONANZA

Rumors of the *Barbie* project were already circulating as Greta was doing interviews and promotion for *Little Women*. Some were puzzled why the writer-director who gave us such beautiful, self-effacing yet strong female characters was going to be reduced to telling the story of a plastic figurine who some believed to be the antithesis of feminism. But as the thought percolated, the tone shifted. Who better than a feminist writer-director to dissect all that the doll represented, and do so with her incredible, didactic yet fun dialogue?

When early production shots of neon-clad Barbie and Ken (aka Margot Robbie and Ryan Gosling) leaked, or when we got the first look at Margot's toe-balanced doll feet, there was a social media feeding frenzy. On TikTok alone, there were nearly one billion views of Barbie-related content before the movie even came out, according to *Elle*.

The topic of *Barbie* famously came up in Greta's *Vogue* cover story in January 2020, though she remained mum on providing too many details at the time, just confirming she'd signed on to write the script and had brought in her go-to partner, Noah Baumbach, to join her. It was also around this time that Noah himself found out—from a headline. Greta "forgot" to tell him. "I think I said, 'Apparently we're writing a movie called *Barbie* . . . I couldn't even fathom it," he said in a *60 Minutes* interview alongside Greta. "And I said, 'Oooh, whoops,'" she jokingly countered.

Noah admitted he "made some calls" to try to get out of it, but the ink was dry, and the months ahead would show that everything happens for a reason, even in Hollywood. "Greta was persistent and Greta saw something," Noah added on *60 Minutes*, alluding to the way his creative partner was able to find rich, compelling storylines—whether human or doll—that resonated with multiple demographics, generations, and viewpoints.

In *Barbie*, that meant not only creating a character and story out of the ether (since Barbie has never really had a full identity), but

Margot Robbie as Barbie in her pink Dreamcar, taken on the film's set in 2022.

THE HOLY FILM TRIFECTA 153

also exploring the very polarizing opinions on who or what the doll represents, from every angle. The film had to appeal to both the people who loved Barbie and those who despised her very existence. But, then again, Greta has always been able to toe the line between disparate audiences.

"There were a lot of questions about, like, should we be saying this or walking into this stuff, but my feeling was, people already know it's a hornet's nest. We cannot make something that pretends to be other than that," she shared in the *60 Minutes* interview. "Barbie has been around since 1959 and everyone knows who she is and everyone has an opinion and she's run the gamut of being ahead of time, behind the times, she's a hero, she's a villain." It was a complexity that thrilled Greta, who shared with *Time*, "If you can tell something personal within that structure, you prove you have command over it."

In many ways, Greta's previous work set her up to dissect Barbie in a cinematic autopsy to get at her heart and soul. Greta not only spent years finding the flaws and grace and humanity in her characters (Lady Bird, Frances Halladay, Brooke Cardinas), but she also reinterpreted very well-known and layered figures of Americana (Josephine March) to give them new life. In *Barbie*, she did both. As she told *Gentlewoman UK*, "It sounds crazy . . . but *Barbie* is not so dissimilar from the process of adapting *Little Women*—I had such a clear sense of what this thing was that I loved and how I wanted to come at it and change it."

The only way to do so was to confront the dichotomy head on. Greta shared with *Rolling Stone* that her idea for the construct of *Barbie* was really going back to the dawn of humankind, tapping into the tale of Adam and Eve in the Garden of Eden (again echoing her belief that biblical stories set the foundation for her narrative exploits). "I started from this idea of Barbieland, this place with no death, no aging, no decay, no pain, no shame. We know the story. We've heard this story . . . What happens to that person? They have to leave. And they have to confront all the things that were shielded from them in this place."

"I started from this idea of Barbieland, this place with no death, no aging, no decay, no pain, no shame. We know the story. We've heard this story . . . What happens to that person? They have to leave. And they have to confront all the things that were shielded from them in this place."

Greta sharing laughs on the 2022 set of *Barbie* with Ryan Gosling, Simu Liu, and Margot Robbie.

Following: Margot Robbie as Barbie taking in the views of Barbieland in a still from the 2023 movie.

THE HOLY FILM TRIFECTA

She added that, in doing so, she was able to find the humanity of the character. "How Barbie operates in Barbieland is she's entirely continuous with her environment. Even the houses have no walls, because you never need to hide because there's nothing to be ashamed of or embarrassed of. And suddenly finding yourself in the real world and wishing you could hide, that's the essence of being human." The most profound part of it all is that *Barbie* begs the question, is it better to live in a state of ignorant bliss or grow from lessons learned the hard way?

Mattel may not have known what they had gotten themselves into when they approved Greta as the film's director. The toy giant, led by CEO Ynon Kreiz, was just looking for a summer blockbuster that could possibly lead to a chain of million-dollar sequels. Barbie dolls had hit a sales slump around 2014–2015 but found new interest during the pandemic as parents tried to find ways to entertain kids stuck at home (per CNN). Mattel wanted to capitalize on that resurgence. Yet they got an existential reckoning packaged up in a movie.

Will Ferrell leading the rollerblading scene in *Barbie*, filmed in Los Angeles, California, June 2022.

Greta sharing a moment with Ryan Gosling while filming *Barbie* on location in Los Angeles, California, June 2022.

THE HOLY FILM TRIFECTA 159

The toy company did have their qualms about some parts of the film, namely a Mattel exec getting shot during the beach fracas, the inclusion of the maligned Allan doll, and dialogue from the teenage character Sasha deeming the dolls fascist and anti-feminist. "It wasn't like I ever got the full seal of approval from [Mattel], like, 'We love it!' I got a tentative, 'Well, okay. I see that you are going to do this, so go ahead and we'll see how it goes,'" Greta told the *New York Times*. "But that's all you need, and I had faith once it was in there and they saw it that they would embrace it, not fight it. Maybe at the end of the day, my will to have it in was stronger than any other will to take it out."

It still worked in Mattel's favor. Sales of the doll jumped nearly 10 percent after the movie's billion-dollar frenzy, according to *Fortune*. All of a sudden, Barbie was compelling again—for many different reasons.

The *Barbie* project was four and a half years in the making, after actress Margot Robbie secured the rights to produce a film about the doll in 2018 through her production company LuckyChap. She's the one

Margot Robbie and Ryan Gosling having fun on the set of the 2023 film *Barbie*.

Opposite: Margot Robbie as Barbie and Ryan Gosling as Ken—the perfect pair—in a still from the 2023 movie.

who specifically sought out Greta to create the story, after seeing her adaptation of *Little Women*. "I definitely didn't want to try and make a puff piece *Barbie*. I wanted us to run at the scary things as much as we celebrated the wonderful things," Margot told *Deadline*. "That's exactly why I went after Greta, because I was like, 'She would do that.'"

Truthfully, Greta did have her hesitations at first, telling the *Guardian* she was "terrified" to sign up for the task of essentially creating *Barbie* out of nothing. "It's not like a superhero, who already has a story. It felt very much like it was going to be an adaptation. Except what we were adapting is a doll—an icon of the 20th century." Yet, the challenge thrilled her: "It felt complicated enough, sticky enough, *strange* enough, that maybe there could be something interesting there to be discovered."

She and Noah got to work on the script during the pandemic, which directly lead to the film's ostentatiousness. "There was this sense of wanting to make something anarchic and wild and completely bananas," she told the *Guardian*, "because it felt, like, 'Well, if we ever do get to go back to cinemas again, let's do something totally unhinged.'"

When the script was finished, Greta recalled she had two looming thoughts. "I love this and I can't bear it if anyone else makes it. And, they'll *never* let us make this movie."

But they did. Warner Bros. and Mattel gave Greta and Noah their blessing, doing so after Greta read executives a poem as her pitch. And they gave their sign-off to have her direct it. Even she couldn't believe they bought into the idea. "There was a moment where I was like, 'Wow, I'm way out there,' like if this doesn't work, it will be . . . very public," Greta told *60 Minutes*, even wondering how it might affect her career if *Barbie* tanked. Luckily, her instincts paid off, not only how she developed the story, but also the greater, over-the-top world around it.

Top: Margot Robbie as Barbie in the opening dance scene from the 2023 film *Barbie*.

Bottom: Margot Robbie as Barbie and Ryan Gosling as Ken going for a joyride in Barbie's Dreamcar in a scene from the 2023 film.

"When I was a little girl, I loved Lisa Frank. I thought her art was the most beautiful thing I'd ever seen. Then as you get older, you say, 'No, I have adult taste, and I don't need sparkle dolphins.' But there is still someone in you that loves a sparkle dolphin. You just have to let them out and play a little bit."

A still taken from the disco-themed dance scene in the 2023 movie *Barbie*.

Opposite: Greta laughing at Weird Barbie and Ken on the set of the 2023 movie *Barbie*.

"One thing we really did think deeply about with the set and costume design was ... not diminishing a little girl that just loves the brightness and the sparkles and the too-muchness," Greta told *W*. "When eight-year-old girls play dress up, they put on everything. When I was a little girl, I loved Lisa Frank. I thought her art was the most beautiful thing I'd ever seen. Then as you get older, you say, 'No, I have adult taste, and I don't need sparkle dolphins.' But there is still someone in you that loves a sparkle dolphin. You just have to let them out and play a little bit."

To that end, Greta did stay true to the branding of Barbie and her Dreamhouse by making the setting a bright, pink paradise that echoes the world of kids playing with toys. It was an interesting side-by-side, keeping the innocence of Barbie's appeal to children while giving the adults in the room the deep meaning they maybe were not expecting. The film opens with Strauss's *Also sprach Zarathustra* (the same composition that plays in Stanley Kubrick's *2001: A Space Odyssey*) soundtracking an oversized Barbie coming to earth. Later in the film, when Barbie talks about death in Barbieland, there's a pronounced record player scratch, as the whole trajectory of the film shifts into real-world dystopia.

Allotted a $100 million-plus production budget, Greta and co. created a whole new world that sucked viewers in, inviting them to marvel at its bombast and contradictions from real life. As *60 Minutes* explains, "*Barbie* has that technicolor soundstage look because Gerwig convinced the studio to build one, complete with a painted sky and backdrop to give the movie a 2D effect." She was given a pink golf cart just to navigate the buildouts, sets that were directly inspired by touring the mythical Mattel Design Center in El Segundo, California. There, the Barbie division is the largest entity on the company campus. The bright pink conference room Greta took meetings in became the blueprint for the fictional corporation she created in the movie and touring hallways covered with photos of the volumes of Barbies from years past gave her the idea to create the community living together in Barbieland.

Greta sharing a laugh with Ryan Gosling on the set of the 2023 film *Barbie*.

    As with all her films, Greta was protective of and attentive to her cast, which in addition to Margot Robbie in the title role included the incredible Ryan Gosling (Greta and Noah manifested him playing Ken by writing his name in their script liner notes early on), America Ferrera, Greta's college improv friend Kate McKinnon, Issa Rae, and plenty of other notables. Margot remembers panicking before filming started, and her director effectively talking her off the ledge. "I went to Greta's house and had that crisis. I'd spent years trying to get this movie going. And suddenly we're going to shoot the thing. And I was like, 'Oh, my God, I dunno how to do this,'" she told the *Los Angeles Times*, about struggling with the blank slate character and how to effectively portray her. "There's nothing here to hold onto, because she doesn't have childhood trauma and she doesn't have all these things that I normally latch onto and then build off. She doesn't have any of it, and I couldn't get her. And then Greta helped me through that and pointed me in all the right directions, and we talked through it."

GRETA

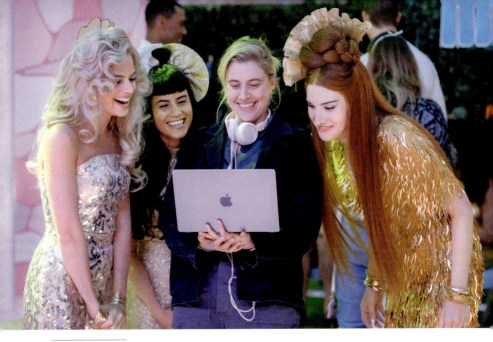

Greta and a wide range of Barbies on the set of the 2023 film.

Barbie was largely filmed at a soundstage outside London, and after shooting days, Greta would often bring the cast to the nearby Electric Cinema for movie outings, essentially bringing her work family into her world. So much of *Barbie*'s dreamland is dotted with distinctly Greta inspirations. From highly orchestrated beach fights to the Kens' ballet dance number (which they were only allotted one day to shoot), there are hints of some of Greta's favorite musicals and movies like *West Side Story*, *Singin' in the Rain*, and *Gentlemen Prefer Blondes*. The crew got into the pastel spirit once a week as well, as Greta told *Gentlewoman UK*, "It was something Margot started: 'On Wednesdays, we wear pink.' Everyone would do it, including the crew."

The cast also spent weeks going through the opening Barbieland choreography, with no words attached, "almost like a silent film." Greta also specifically zeroed in on that famous "not good enough" speech by America Ferrera's character Gloria; after just three takes (of about fifty), Greta found herself and everyone on the crew crying. A passionate monologue is one of her movie hallmarks and is perhaps its finest in *Barbie*, almost like a "writer's version of a guitar solo," hailed *60 Minutes*.

"Honestly, the whole movie, when I watch it, I still can't believe anybody let me do this," Greta said in that interview. But the risk paid off. *Barbie* was an enormous success, the likes of which had not been seen in many years. It ranks in the top 15 highest-grossing films of all time, was the biggest money maker for Warner Bros. ever, and Greta is, so far, the only solo female director to cross the $1 billion threshold (the other moviemaker who got close was Patty Jenkins for her 2017 *Wonder Woman* movie, which netted $822 million). It sparked a Barbiecore movement—you couldn't go two blocks without seeing a pop of pink in the summer of 2023. And it also changed perceptions on not only what Greta was capable of, but also what all the other women in her field could do if given the same opportunity and access.

Of course, *Barbie* didn't come without its controversy. Some dubbed the film man-hating; Shakira even publicly called it emasculating. Conservatives, in particular, rallied around their take that the film represented an "assault on men." But that was par for the course—it was a woman taking on the patriarchy. "I felt men could take it," said Noah in the *60 Minutes* interview. And truly it was a soft yelp that was drowned out in all the buzz.

Reviews were also mixed, though predominately favorable. The *New Yorker* hailed *Barbie* as "brilliant, beautiful, and fun as hell," while *America* magazine said it was "a film by women, about women, for women," and the *Independent* declared in its five-star review, "*Barbie* is one of the most inventive, immaculately crafted, and surprising mainstream films in recent memory." But then there were outlets like *Time*, who called the film "very pretty but not very deep," and the *New*

Greta with her Barbie cast (America Ferrera, Simu Liu, Margot Robbie, Issa Rae, and Ryan Gosling) on the red carpet at a premiere in London, July 2023.

York Times*, who printed an opinion piece that stated, " '*Barbie*' is bad. There, I said it."

There was another stab felt 'round the world when Greta—and Margot—did not get their due with proper Best Director and Best Actress nominations, respectively, at the 2024 Academy Awards. Adding salt to the wound was the fact that Greta and Noah's Best Screenplay nod was lumped into the "adapted" rather than "original" category, especially as the BAFTAs, Critics' Choice Awards, and Writers Guild of America included *Barbie*'s script in their "original" categories.

Margot shared with the *Los Angeles Times*, "As a producer and her actor, would I have loved to see Greta nominated for directing? Of course . . . She cracked the code on this film, as only she could. It is such a singular vision, and Greta brought so much humanity, creativity, inspiration, magic, and joy to *Barbie*. And it's because of her we've all received such acclaim." For Greta's part, she told *Time*, "I'm just happy we all get to be there together [at the Oscars]."

Barbie was a record-breaking success and put Greta in the big leagues of mainstream movies. It was also another project complete, with lessons learned that can be carried over into the next one. "In terms of my own future, I definitely want the skill set to be able to tell stories of different sizes. I want to be able to make tiny movies, big movies, and everything in between," she told *W*. "It just takes so long to make any given one. That's the only thing I feel limited by. You only get to make so many."

Top: Greta and Margot Robbie receiving the award for Cinematic and Box Office Achievement for Barbie at the 81st Golden Globe Awards in Los Angeles, California, January 2024.

Bottom: Greta on the red carpet at the 77th Cannes Film Festival, where she served as president of the jury, in France, May 2024.

Following: Greta, wearing pink headphones, taking a moment on the set of the 2023 film *Barbie*.

THE HOLY FILM TRIFECTA

"In terms of my own future, I definitely want the skill set to be able to tell stories of different sizes. I want to be able to make tiny movies, big movies, and everything in between. It just takes so long to make any given one. That's the only thing I feel limited by. You only get to make so many."

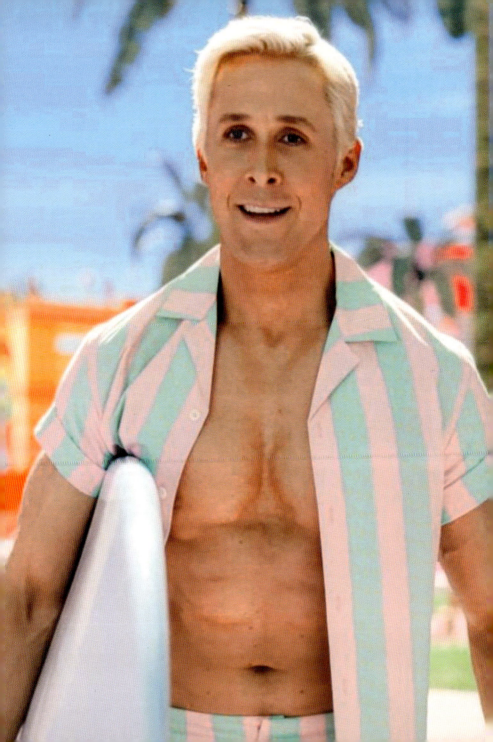

Greta's World
Ken

In the *Barbie* movie—and, really, in all of Barbie playtime—Kens are seen as not much more than accessories to the leading lady doll, flipping the real world's idea of trophy wives on its head. But both Greta and Noah felt that Ken's perspective was an important part of their story, and they wanted to give him a voice too. "There was something really early when Noah and I were working on [the script]—Ken as an accessory and how forgotten he is—we just felt, psychologically: That's going to be the story. There's [a] story there. How could there not be?" Greta told the *Los Angeles Times*.

In the movie, Ken (played by Ryan Gosling, in one of his best roles ever) goes through just as much of a revelation as Barbie when he realizes that there is such a thing as patriarchy and wants his due when they return to Barbieland. He gets his own theme song, choreographed dance, and now popular catchphrase, "I Am Kenough," that piggybacks on the feelings expressed by women. Greta's proliferation of female characters clearly came into play with the making of Ken. He's vulnerable and anxious and much more dimensional than the tanned, buff, beach himbo we often come to regard him as.

Ryan, a father of two girls who famously texted Greta a picture of a Ken doll he found in his backyard as his acceptance of the role, told the *Los Angeles Times,* "There was such a synergy between what I was watching happening in my own house and then also the brilliance in the way that Greta was using these characters to do something similar. I walked into my backyard and I saw Ken laying facedown in the mud next to a squished lemon. And I thought, she's right. This story does have to be told."

Ryan Gosling taking his role of Ken seriously on the set of the 2023 film *Barbie*.

Following: The infamous beach battle scene in the 2023 film *Barbie*.

Take 5

The Future Is Waiting

"I live really close to the New School and New York University, and these younger women come up to me and say, 'I saw your film and I want to make my own films.' Being recognized by my peers in the Academy, and then having that translate to young women directly—it's the reason I do it."

—Greta talking to *Time* in 2019

Greta Gerwig's success in recent years is excellent evidence that the future is most certainly female. *Barbie*'s massive blitz came at an uncanny time in American history, sandwiched between the fight for reproductive rights and women's bodily autonomy and the ongoing fight to elect the country's first female president. The film also proved why women, people of color, and non-binary moviemakers unequivocally matter and create stories that provide perspective and

---

Greta standing out on the red carpet at the 77th Cannes Film Festival in France, May 2024.

understanding for all of us—if not also sway the future. We're not saying Barbieland's woman president had anything to do with Kamala Harris becoming the Democratic candidate in the 2024 presidential election, but we're not saying it didn't either.

Cannes got the memo when, in May 2024, they selected Greta to be the first female American director to serve as the jury president for the film festival in its nearly eighty-year history. In press materials, Cannes highlighted Greta's incredibly unique career trajectory over the past two decades, a fraction of the time it takes most moviemakers to reach her level: "Yesterday, ambassador of independent American cinema, today at the summit of worldwide box-office success, Greta Gerwig manages to combine what was previously judged to be incompatible: delivering arthouse blockbusters, narrowing the gap between art and industry, exploring contemporary feminist issues with deft as well as depth, and declaring her demanding artistic ambition from within an economic model that she embraces in order to put to better use."

Calling her a "heroine for modern times" and the "future of cinema," Cannes president Iris Knobloch's decision to pick Greta as jury president dovetailed with Iris' own unprecedented appointment as the in 2022, the first time a woman had ever held that role and coming amidst scrutiny that Cannes had not done its part to level the playing field. "I feel that defending the cause of women is a big part of my role," Iris shared with the *Guardian*. "We can see the progress being made, with many more films [by women] coming in and more women speaking up. That's why having Greta Gerwig as jury president is so important."

Greta echoed that sentiment in her own response in the article. "I've been making movies for almost twenty years, and this has never not been a question: increasing the number of female directors," she said. "In my lifetime it's changed and gotten better. Every year I cheer because there are more women directors. We're not done yet, but we are certainly moving in the right direction. It's all about the long arc of history."

Greta looking regal while walking up the stairs at 77th Cannes Film Festival in France, May 2024.

"I've been making movies for almost twenty years, and this has never not been a question: increasing the number of female directors. In my lifetime it's changed and gotten better. Every year I cheer because there are more women directors. We're not done yet, but we are certainly moving in the right direction. It's all about the long arc of history."

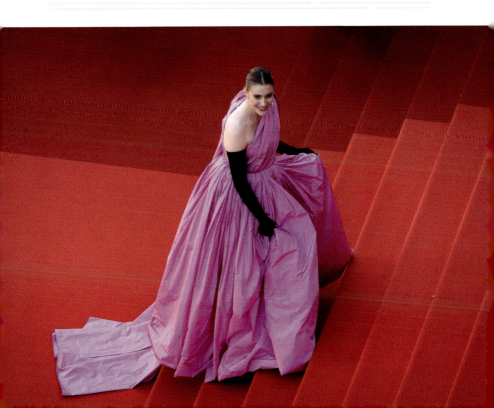

As of 2023, the number of women making "top-grossing movies" stood at a stark 14 percent of the top 100 films of all-time, according to the Women In Film organization, while USC studies have found that among current filmmakers, "men still outrank their female counterparts 20 to 1." But it wasn't always that way. The book *Early Women Directors* by Anthony Slide says that women "dominated the industry" in the silent film era and "were considered equal to, if not better than, their male colleagues," per an excerpt of the book in *Forbes*.

So, why, in the twenty-first century, more than 125 years since the first female film director, Alice Guy-Blaché, directed 1896's *La Fée aux Choux*, is there still such a divide? The answers are multi-fold but can, in the simplest terms, boil down to studio directors who tend to "go with what's working" (i.e. largely male directors) and up-and-coming women who don't often see representation in the field. Greta Gerwig is a one-woman response to both of those demands: With a record-breaking $1.45 billion-making movie and her face plastered everywhere as the woman behind it all, her work far exceeds mere entertainment and is no doubt going to change the course of cinematic history.

You can already see that change unfolding among those in her inner orbit. Margot Robbie told *Variety* in January 2024 that "directing is a dear ambition of mine." Her company, LuckyChap, makes it a point to collaborate with women directors, not only Greta but also Emerald Fennell and Olivia Wilde. When it comes to Greta, in particular, Margot told *Gentlewoman UK*, "She understands people and cares about people in a way I've never seen other directors do. But she's also a true film lover. She has such a reverence for the filmmakers of the past but also has her finger on the pulse of the world we live in today."

Saoirse Ronan is also under Greta's spell, not only coming back to the fold as an actor on two of Greta's projects but also now feeling the impulse to try out the director's chair. As she told *Entertainment Weekly*, "The director is who I always loved the most . . . It's something that I would absolutely love to do and yeah, it's just because I've picked

"I think I'm prematurely worrying about this, but I want to make movies up until my eighties, and working as a director is a very physical thing."

up so many things from other directors that I've worked with. Watching Greta, and seeing what she's done over the last few years, has been a massive motivation for me to give it a go."

In a side-by-side interview with the *Hollywood Reporter*, Saoirse and Greta vowed to become "old ladies together making movies about old ladies." Greta has already thought about sticking it out for the long haul, telling *Gentlewoman UK* that she's added more workouts to her routine to stay healthy enough to keep making movies in her golden years: "I think I'm prematurely worrying about this, but I want to make movies up until my eighties, and working as a director is a very physical thing."

As for what's ahead, Greta has signed on to helm a new *Chronicles of Narnia* adaptation for Netflix; she has been tapped to write and direct two of the books in C. S. Lewis' beloved series. Like *Little Women* before *Lady Bird*, she started working on the *Chronicles of Narnia* project before *Barbie*.

"I'm slightly in the place of terror because I really do have such reverence for Narnia. I loved Narnia so much as a child . . . I'm intimidated by doing this. It's something that feels like a worthy thing to be intimidated by," she admitted to the BBC in early 2024, adding, "As a non-British person, I feel a particular sense of wanting to do it correctly . . . it's like when Americans do Shakespeare, there's a slight feeling of reverence and as if maybe we should treat it with extra care. It is not our countryman." Early reports said production would begin in August 2024 in the UK, though there is no confirmed release schedule as of this writing.

Greta also had limited involvement in Disney's new live-action *Snow White*. As she told *Screen Daily*, "I was hired for a couple weeks. I did a 'pass'—I wrote some jokes."

As for what the long-term future holds, it's anyone's guess, even Greta's. The only certainty is that she will keep working and evolving and impressing audiences. "I would love to make an original movie musical," she told *Gentlewoman UK*. *Vogue* said Greta's been in talks with *Little Women* producer Amy Pascal about doing just that, adding Greta "keeps a list of future project ideas on her iPhone and in the pages of brightly colored Smythson notebooks."

Wherever Greta's next projects take her, women are certain to keep taking a huge focus. "I like writing about women in relation to other women—mothers and daughters, friends, sisters, mentors, employees and employers, et cetera—because men don't know what women do when they aren't there," she told *Bust*. "These are powerful, complicated, rich relationships that deserve their own place in the collection of stories we tell ourselves about what it means to be human."

Greta at the EE British Academy Film Awards Dinner & After Party in London, England, February 2020.

Following: Greta attending the 90th Annual Academy Awards in Los Angeles, California, March 2018.

"I like writing about women in relation to other women—mothers and daughters, friends, sisters, mentors, employees and employers, et cetera—because men don't know what women do when they aren't there. These are powerful, complicated, rich relationships that deserve their own place in the collection of stories we tell ourselves about what it means to be human."

Greta on the set of *Barbie*, 2023.

Filmography

ACTING

2006
LOL (Role: Greta)

2007
Hannah Takes the Stairs (Role: Hannah)

2008
Baghead (Role: Michelle)
Yeast (Role: Gen)
Nights and Weekends (Role: Mattie)
I Thought You Finally Completely Lost It (Role: Greta)

2009
You Won't Miss Me (Role: Bridget)
The House of the Devil (Role: Megan)
Une aventure New-Yorkaise (Role: Tamera)

2010
Greenberg (Role: Florence Marr)
Art House (Role: Nora Ohr)
Northern Comfort (Role: Cassandra)

2011
No Strings Attached (Role: Patrice)
The Dish & the Spoon (Role: Rose)
Arthur (Role: Naomi)
Damsels in Distress (Role: Violet)

2012
To Rome With Love (Role: Sally)
Lola Versus (Role: Lola)

2013
Frances Ha (Role: Frances Halladay)

2014
The Humbling (Role: Pegeen)
Eden (Role: Julia)

2015
Mistress America (Role: Brooke Cardinas)
Portlandia (Role: Mermaid)
China, IL (Voice: Pony Merks)
Maggie's Plan (Role: Maggie Hardin)

2016
Wiener-Dog (Role: Dawn Wiener)
The Mindy Project (Role: Sarah Branum)
Jackie (Role: Nancy Tuckerman)
20th Century Women (Role: Abbie Porter)

2018
Isle of Dogs (Voice: Tracy Walker)

2022
White Noise (Role: Babette)

WRITING

2007
Hannah Takes the Stairs

2008
Nights and Weekends

2010
Northern Comfort

2011
The Dish & the Spoon

2013
Frances Ha

2015
Mistress America
China, IL

2017
Lady Bird

2019
Little Women

2023
Barbie

TBD
The Chronicles of Narnia

DIRECTING

2008
Nights and Weekends

2017
Lady Bird

2019
Little Women

2023
Barbie
Dua Lipa's **"Dance The Night"** music video

TBD
The Chronicles of Narnia

Awards and Nominations

ACADEMY AWARDS

2018: Best Director, *Lady Bird* (Nominated)
2018: Best Original Screenplay, *Lady Bird* (Nominated)
2020: Best Adapted Screenplay, *Little Women* (Nominated)
2024: Best Adapted Screenplay, *Barbie* (Nominated)
*In 2018, *Lady Bird* was also nominated for Best Picture
*In 2020, *Little Women* was also nominated for Best Picture
*In 2024, *Barbie* was also nominated for Best Picture

BAFTA AWARDS

2018: Best Original Screenplay, *Lady Bird* (Nominated)
2020: Best Adapted Screenplay, *Little Women* (Nominated)
2024: Best Original Screenplay, *Barbie* (Nominated)

GOLDEN GLOBE AWARDS

2014: Best Performance by an Actress in a Motion Picture—Musical or Comedy, *Frances Ha* (Nominated)
2018: Best Screenplay—Motion Picture, *Lady Bird* (Nominated)
2024: Best Director—Motion Picture, *Barbie* (Nominated)
2024: Best Screenplay—Motion Picture, *Barbie* (Nominated)
2024: Cinematic and Box Office Achievement, *Barbie* (Won)
*In 2018, *Lady Bird* also won Best Motion Picture—Musical or Comedy
*In 2024, *Barbie* was also nominated for Best Motion Picture—Musical or Comedy

CRITICS' CHOICE MOVIE AWARDS

2014: Best Actress in a Comedy, *Frances Ha* (Nominated)
2017: Best Supporting Actress, *20th Century Women* (Nominated)
2018: Best Director, *Lady Bird* (Nominated)
2018: Best Original Screenplay, *Lady Bird* (Nominated)
2020: Best Director, *Little Women* (Nominated)
2020: Best Adapted Screenplay, *Little Women* (Won)
2024: Best Director, *Barbie* (Nominated)
2024: Best Original Screenplay, *Barbie* (Won)
*In 2018, *Lady Bird* was also nominated for Best Picture
*In 2020, *Little Women* was also nominated for Best Picture
*In 2024, *Barbie* was also nominated for Best Picture

DIRECTORS GUILD OF AMERICA AWARDS

2018: Outstanding Directing—Feature Film, *Lady Bird* (Nominated)
2024: Outstanding Directing—Feature Film, *Barbie* (Nominated)

INDEPENDENT SPIRIT AWARDS

2011: Best Female Lead, *Greenberg* (Nominated)
2018: Best Screenplay, *Lady Bird* (Won)
*In 2018, *Lady Bird* was also nominated for Best Feature

NATIONAL BOARD OF REVIEW

2018: Best Director, *Lady Bird* (Won)

WRITERS GUILD OF AMERICA AWARDS

2018: Best Original Screenplay, *Lady Bird* (Nominated)
2020: Best Adapted Screenplay, *Little Women* (Nominated)
2024: Best Original Screenplay, *Barbie* (Nominated)

Sources

60 Minutes interview, December 2023: https://www.cbsnews.com/news/barbie-filmmaker-greta-gerwig-60-minutes-transcript/

ABC 10, "Greta Gerwig on missing Sacramento and 'Barbie' success," December 2023: https://www.youtube.com/watch?v=r6ASgCTbNkw

Associated Press, "Greta Gerwig snubbed for best director and other Oscar nominations surprises," January 2024: https://apnews.com/article/oscars-2024-snubs-surprises-greta-gerwig-058dc4579a1e059090bd86493f8098d3

Bust, "Greta The Great," December January 2018: https://bust.com/pdfs/greatDames2.pdf

CBS Sunday Morning, "Greta Gerwig on why she fell in love with Barnard College," January 2018: https://www.youtube.com/watch?v=X-9injJxTBD4

Elle, "It's Greta's World . . . The Director Talks Boiler Suits, New Babies, And Barbie-Mania," July 2023: https://www.elle.com/uk/life-and-culture/a44525742/greta-gerwig-barbie-digital-cover/

Entertainment Weekly, "Golden Globes: 'Frances Ha' star Greta Gerwig is 'just very happy right now. I can't make sense!'" December 2013: https://ew.com/article/2013/12/12/golden-globes-frances-ha-greta-gerwig/

Entertainment Weekly, "Greta Gerwig can't stop crying over *Lady Bird*'s Oscar nominations," January 2018: https://ew.com/oscars/2018/01/23/lady-bird-greta-gerwig-reaction-oscar-nominations/

Greta celebrating the Met Gala theme "Sleeping Beauties: Reawakening Fashion," May 2024.

Entertainment Weekly, "Saoirse Ronan says Greta Gerwig 'has been a massive motivation' for her to direct," January 2020: https://ew.com/movies/2020/01/04/little-women-saoirse-ronan-direct-greta-gerwig-motivation/

Forbes, "Greta Gerwig's 'Barbie' Sets A Box Office Record. Here's What It Means For Female Directors," August 2023: https://www.forbes.com/sites/kimelsesser/2023/07/24/greta-gerwig-set-a-box-office-record-heres-what-it-means-for-future-female-directors/

Gentlewoman UK, "Greta Gerwig On bringing little women to big screens," Spring/Summer 2023: https://thegentlewoman.co.uk/library/greta-gerwig

Guardian, "Greta Gerwig: 'I don't need a man. I would have done all this anyway'," August 2015: https://www.theguardian.com/film/2015/aug/06/greta-gerwig-i-dont-need-a-man-i-would-have-done-all-this-anyway

Guardian, "'It had to be totally bananas': Greta Gerwig on bringing Barbie to life," July 2023: https://www.theguardian.com/film/2023/jul/09/it-had-to-be-totally-bananas-greta-gerwig-on-bringing-barbie-back-to-life

Guardian, "Greta Gerwig: 'The number of female directors has gotten better. We're not done yet'," May 2024: https://www.theguardian.com/film/article/2024/may/14/greta-gerwig-cannes-film-festival-female-directors-jury-president

Hollywood Reporter, "Awards Chatter' Podcast — Greta Gerwig ('20th Century Women')," December 2016: https://www.hollywoodreporter.com/news/general-news/awards-chatter-podcast-greta-gerwig-20th-century-women-957298/

IndieWire, "Becoming 'Lady Bird': Greta Gerwig Reflects on 8 Life-Changing Moments That Made Her a Director," November 2017: https://www.indiewire.com/awards/industry/lady-bird-greta-gerwig-writer-director-mojo-oscars-1201893321/

IndieWire, "Female Filmmaking Firsts: 8 Directors Whose Achievements Opened Doors for Women Behind the Camera," August 2023: https://www.indiewire.com/gallery/female-film-directors-history-milestones-hollywood/pbdalgu-ec031/

Interview Magazine, "America's alt-sweetheart Greta Gerwig talks to cinema legend Francis Ford Coppola," November 2017: https://www.interviewmagazine.com/film/greta-gerwig-francis-ford-coppola-lady-bird

Los Angeles Times, "Ryan Gosling and Greta Gerwig on how Ken became the subversive center of 'Barbie'," July 2023: https://www.latimes.com/entertainment-arts/movies/story/2023-07-11/greta-gerwig-ryan-gosling-ken-barbie

Los Angeles Times, "How Margot Robbie overcame a 'palpable and debilitating' panic to make 'Barbie'," February 2024: https://www.latimes.com/entertainment-arts/awards/story/2024-02-05/greta-gerwig-margot-robbie-barbie-oscar-nominations

New Yorker, "Happiness," April 2013: https://www.newyorker.com/magazine/2013/04/29/happiness-don-delillo

New York Magazine, "Sweetheart of Early-Adult Angst," March 2010: https://nymag.com/movies/features/64475/

New York Post, "How Greta Gerwig's 'Barbie' was influenced by her Catholic school roots," July 2023: https://nypost.com/2023/07/21/how-greta-gerwigs-barbie-was-influenced-by-her-catholic-school-roots/

New York Times, "Greta Gerwig: My Mother, My City," January 2018: https://www.nytimes.com/2018/01/04/movies/greta-gerwig-lady-bird-new-york.html

New York Times, "This Is 'Little Women' for a New Era," January 2020: https://www.nytimes.com/2020/01/02/books/little-women-feminism-2019-movie.html

New York Times, "Greta Gerwig on the Blockbuster 'Barbie' Opening (and How She Got Away With It)," July 2023: https://www.nytimes.com/2023/07/25/movies/greta-gerwig-barbie-movie.html

New York Times, "Why Was Greta Gerwig Snubbed for a Best Director Nomination?" January 2024: https://www.nytimes.com/2024/01/23/movies/greta-gerwig-barbie-oscar-snub.html

NPR, "Gerwig, Baumbach Poke At Post-College Pangs," May 2013: https://www.npr.org/transcripts/183648078

NPR, "Greta Gerwig Explores Mother-Daughter Love (And Angst) In 'Lady Bird'," November 2017: https://www.npr.org/transcripts/564579012?storyId=564579012?storyId=564579012

NPR, "Greta Gerwig On Her 'Little Women' Film Adaptation," December 2019: https://www.npr.org/2019/12/22/790631863/greta-gerwig-on-her-little-women-film-adaptation

Paste, "Greta Gerwig and Joe Swanberg: The Penny-Pinching Future of Indie Cinema," March 2009: https://www.pastemagazine.com/movies/greta-gerwig/greta-gerwig-and-joe-swanberg-the-penny-pinching-future-of-indie-cinema

People, "Greta Gerwig and Kate McKinnon Made 'Strange Musicals' Together in College Years Before 'Barbie' (Exclusive)," July 2023: https://people.com/greta-gerwig-and-kate-mckinnon-made-strange-musicals-together-in-college-years-before-barbie-exclusive-7565662

Rolling Stone, "The Brain Behind 'Barbie': Inside the Brilliant Mind of Greta Gerwig," July 2023: https://www.rollingstone.com/tv-movies/tv-movie-features/barbie-greta-gerwig-interview-margot-robbie-ryan-gosling-superhero-movie-1234769344/

Sacramento Bee, "Will someone help Greta Gerwig make her ode to Sacramento?" April 2016: https://www.sacbee.com/opinion/opn-columns-blogs/shawn-hubler/article69510342.html

Sactown Magazine, Q&A, April-May 2010: https://www.sactownmag.com/greta-gerwig/

Teen Vogue, "President Barbie Issa Rae Drew Inspiration From Kamala Harris for *Barbie* Movie, July 2023: https://www.teenvogue.com/story/barbie-issa-rae-interview

Time 100, 2018 feature: "Greta Gerwig by Steven Spielberg" https://time.com/collection/most-influential-people-2018/5217536/greta-gerwig-2/

Variety, "Greta Gerwig talks why she moved to New York," December 2016: https://www.youtube.com/watch?v=hiDAK1dKZgc

Variety, "Patty Jenkins, Greta Gerwig Detail Why Women Make Great Directors," November 2017: https://variety.com/2017/scene/news/patty-jenkins-greta-gerwig-women-directors-wonder-woman-1202606176/

Variety, "Margot Robbie & LuckyChap's Entertainment Empire: How They're Thriving Off 'Barbie,' 'Saltburn' Shocks and 'Being Original Every Time'," January 2024: https://variety.com/2024/film/features/margot-robbie-luckychap-barbie-saltburn-shocks-being-original-1235858528/

VICE, "Greta Gerwig and Saoirse Ronan Know 'Lady Bird' Is Extraordinary," November 2017: https://www.vice.com/en/article/xwa5qj/greta-gerwig-and-saoirse-ronan-know-lady-bird-is-extraordinary

Vogue, "Greta Gerwig on the Twin Adventures of Filmmaking and Motherhood," December 2019: https://www.vogue.com/article/greta-gerwig-cover-january-2020

Vulture, "Mumblecore Muse Greta Gerwig on 'Nights and Weekends' and the Ugly Side of Movie Sex," October 2008: https://www.vulture.com/2008/10/mumblecore_muse_greta_gerwig_0.html

W Magazine, "How Greta Gerwig Brought Indie Spirit to *Barbie*," July 2023: https://www.wmagazine.com/culture/greta-gerwig-barbie-interview

Photo Credits

p. 2 Dimitrios Kambouris/Getty Images Entertainment/Getty Images North America. **p. 4-5** Francois Durand/Stringer/Getty Images Entertainment/Getty Images Europe. **p. 6** Mike Marsland/WireImage/Getty Images. **p. 9** Mattel Films/Entertainment Pictures/Alamy Stock Photo. **p. 11** Warner Bros./Album/Alamy Stock Photo. **p. 12** MEGA/GC Images/Getty Images. **p. 15** Toni Passig/WireImage/Getty Images. **p. 16** Iona Wolff/BAFTA/Getty Images. **p. 18** Warner Bros/Entertainment Pictures/Alamy Stock Photos. **p. 20** Nicky Nelson/WENN/Alamy Stock Photos. **p. 21** Collection Christophel/Alamy Stock Photo. **p. 22** Fairchild Archive/Penske Media/Getty Images. **p. 33** Scott Rudin Productions/ Album/Alamy Stock Photo. **p. 35** Collection Christophel/Alamy Stock Photo. **p. 36** Rob Latour/Variety/Penske Media/Getty Images. **p. 38** Cinematic/Alamy Stock Photo. **p. 41** Collection Christophel/Alamy Stock Photo. **p. 42** Collection Christophel/Alamy Stock Photo. **p. 43** TCD/Prod.DB/Alamy Stock Photo **p. 44** Scott Rudin Productions/Album/Alamy Stock Photo. **p. 46** Everett Collection Inc/Alamy Stock Photo. **p. 57** Emma McIntyre/Getty Images Entertainment/Getty Images North America. **p. 59** Collection Christophel/Alamy Stock Photo. **p. 63** WENN Rights Ltd/Alamy Stock Photo. **p. 67** Emma McIntyre/Getty Images Entertainment/Getty Images North America. **p. 68** Photo12/7e Art/Wilson Webb/Columbia Pictures/Alamy Stock Photo. **p. 70** Photo12/7e Art/Wilson Webb/Columbia Pictures/Alamy Stock Photo. **p. 71** Entertainment Pictures/Alamy Stock Photo. **p. 72-73** TCD/Prod.DB/Alamy Stock Photo. **p. 74** Scott Gries/Getty Images Entertainment/Getty Images North America. **p. 76** TCD/Prod.DB/Alamy Stock Photo. **p. 78** Maximum Film/Alamy Stock Photo. **p. 81** Michael Robinson Chavez/Los Angeles Times/Getty Images. **p. 82** Collection Christophel/Alamy Stock Photo. **p. 83** Cinematic/Alamy Stock Photo. **p. 85** Gareth Cattermole/Getty Images Entertainment/Getty Images Europe. **p. 86** Jim Ruymen/UPI/Alamy Live News/ Alamy Stock Photo. **p. 89** dpa picture alliance archive/Alamy Stock Photo. **p. 90** dpa picture alliance/Alamy Stock Photo. **p. 91** Gareth Cattermole/Getty Images Entertainment/Getty Images Europe. **p. 92** Pictorial Press Ltd/Alamy Stock Photo. **p. 93** Fox Searchlight Pictures/Photo 12/Alamy Stock Photo. **p. 94** Andrew H. Walker/Getty Images Entertainment/Getty Images North America. **p. 95** (above) Rommel Demano/Stringer/Getty Images Entertainment/Getty Images North America. **p. 95** (below) Cinematic Collection/Alamy Stock Photo. **p. 97** Sony Pictures Classics/Cinematic Collection/Alamy Stock Photo. **p. 98** Pictorial Press Ltd/Alamy Stock Photo. **p. 100** WFPA/Alamy Stock Photo. **p. 102** Vittorio Zunino Celotto/Getty Images Entertainment/Getty Images Europe. **p. 103** Pictorial Press Ltd/Alamy Stock Photo. **p. 106** Pine District Pictures/Photo 12/Alamy Stock Photo. **p. 108** Moviestore Collection Ltd/Alamy Stock Photo. **p. 109** (above) TCD/Prod.DB/Alamy Stock Photo. **p. 109** (below)

Alberto E. Rodriguez/Getty Images Entertainment/Getty Images North America. **p. 111** TCD/Prod.DB/Alamy Stock Photo. **p. 112** Warner Bros./Album/Alamy Stock Photo. **p. 115** PictureLux/The Hollywood Archive/Alamy Stock Photo. **p. 118** Merie Wallace; Scott Rudin Productions/Photo 12/Alamy Stock Photo. **p. 119** Collection Christophel/Alamy Stock Photo. **p. 121** (above) Collection Christophel/Alamy Stock Photo. **p. 121** (below) Merie Wallace; Scott Rudin Productions/Photo 12/Alamy Stock Photo. **p. 123** Scott Rudin Productions/Album/Alamy Stock Photo. **p. 125** Merie Wallace; Scott Rudin Productions/Photo 12/Alamy Stock Photo. **p. 129** Merie Wallace; Scott Rudin Productions/Photo 12/Alamy Stock Photo. **p. 131** Merie Wallace; Scott Rudin Productions/Photo 12/Alamy Stock Photo. **p. 133** Rob Latour/Variety/Penske Media/Getty Images. **p. 134** Paul Drinkwater/NBCUniversal Handout/Getty Images Entertainment/Getty Images North America. **p. 136** (above) Photo12/7e Art/Wilson Webb/Columbia Pictures/Alamy Stock Photo. **p. 136** (below) Columbia Pictures/Entertainment Pictures/Alamy Stock Photo. **p. 138** Photo12/7e Art/Wilson Webb/Columbia Pictures/Alamy Stock Photo. **p. 140** Collection Christophel/Alamy Stock Photo. **p. 141** Columbia Pictures/Album/Alamy Stock Photo. **p. 143** Photo12/7e Art/Wilson Webb/Columbia Pictures/Alamy Stock Photo. **p. 145** (above) Lifestyle pictures/Alamy Stock Photo. **p. 145** (below) Columbia Pictures/Album/Alamy Stock Photo. **p. 147** Photo12/7e Art/Wilson Webb/Columbia Pictures/Alamy Stock Photo. **p. 148** (above) Columbia Pictures/Album/Alamy Stock Photo. **p. 148** (below) Paul Marotta/Stringer/Getty Images Entertainment/Getty Images North America. **p. 151** Tim P.Whitby/Stringer/Getty Images Entertainment/Getty Images Europe. **p. 152** Warner Bros./Entertainment Pictures/Zumapress.com/Alamy Stock Photo. **p. 155** Warner Bros/Entertainment Pictures/ Alamy Stock Photo. **p. 156-157** Warner Bros/Entertainment Pictures/Alamy Stock Photo. **p. 158** MEGA/GC Images/Getty Images. **p. 159** Bellocqimages/Bauer-Griffin/GC Images/Getty Images. **p. 160** Warner Bros./Album/Alamy Stock Photo. **p. 161** TCD/Prod.DB/Alamy Stock Photo. **p. 162** (above) Moviestore Collection Ltd/Alamy Stock Photo. **p. 162** (below) BFA/Warner Bros/Alamy Stock Photo. **p. 166** TCD/Prod.DB/Alamy Stock Photo. **p. 16**7 Warner Bros./Album/Alamy Stock Photo. **p. 168** Warner Bros./Album/Alamy Stock Photo. **p. 169** Warner Bros./Album/Alamy Stock Photo. **p. 171** David M. Benett/Jed Cullen/Dave Benett/WireImage/Getty Images. **p. 172** (above) PMC/Alamy Live News/Alamy Stock Photo. **p. 172** (below) Barbara Thiem/Alamy Stock Photo. **p. 174** Warner Bros./Album/Alamy Stock Photo. **p. 176** Pictorial Press Ltd/Alamy Stock Photo. **p. 178-179** TCD/P+E104rod.DB/Alamy Stock Photo. **p. 180** Samir Hussein/WireImage/Getty Images. **p. 183** Stephane Cardinale/Corbis Entertainment/Getty Images. **p. 187** Carlo Paloni/BAFTA/Getty Images. **p. 189** Christopher Polk/Getty Images Entertainment/Getty Images North America. **p. 190** Warner Bros./Album/Alamy Stock Photo. **p. 192** Aliah Anderson/Getty Images Entertainment/Getty Images North America. **p. 202** Victor Boyko/Stringer/Getty Images Entertainment/Getty Images Europe. **p. 204** Matthias Nareyek/Getty Images Entertainment/Getty Images Europe.

Acknowledgments

To my mother, Christine, and the beautiful and complex mother-daughter relationship that could be its own movie. Thank you for recognizing the Lady Bird fire in me from a young age and never trying to extinguish my spirit.

Greta walking the red carpet of the closing ceremony at the 77th annual Cannes Film Festival; she served as President of the Jury for this year's festival, May 2024.

About the Author

Selena Fragassi is an entertainment journalist with more than fifteen years of experience and plenty of stories to tell (though she only wishes she could do so with half the grace of Greta Gerwig). A regular contributor for the *Chicago Sun-Times*, she also previously wrote *New Kids On The Block 40th Anniversary Celebration* and *NSYNC 30th Anniversary Celebration* for Quarto/Epic Ink and has contributed to the *Spooky America* series for Arcadia Publishing. Her byline has also appeared in *SPIN*, *Loudwire*, *The A.V. Club*, *Paste*, *Nylon*, *PopMatters*, *Blurt*, *Under the Radar*, and *Chicago Magazine*, where she was previously on staff as the Pop/Rock Music Critic. Selena's work has been anthologized in *That Devil Music: Best Music Writing* and she has appeared on televised panels for WTTW's *Chicago Tonight*. She is also a member of the Recording Academy.

Greta during the 68th Berlinale International Film Festival, February 2018.

© 2025 by Quarto Publishing Group USA Inc.

First published in 2025 by Epic Ink, an imprint of The Quarto Group,
142 West 36th Street, 4th Floor, New York, NY 10018, USA
(212) 779-4972 • www.Quarto.com

All rights reserved. No part of this book may be reproduced in any form without written
permission of the copyright owners. All images included in this book are original
works created by the artist credited on the copyright page, not generated by artificial
intelligence, and have been reproduced with the knowledge and prior consent of the artist.
The producer, publisher, and printer accept no responsibility for any infringement of
copyright or otherwise arising from the contents of this publication. Every effort has been
made to ensure that credits accurately comply with information supplied. We apologize
for any inaccuracies that may have occurred and will resolve inaccurate or missing
information in a subsequent reprinting of the book.

Epic Ink titles are also available at discount for retail, wholesale, promotional, and bulk
purchase. For details, contact the Special Sales Manager by email at specialsales@quarto.com
or by mail at The Quarto Group, Attn: Special Sales Manager, 100 Cummings Center Suite
265D, Beverly, MA 01915 USA.

10 9 8 7 6 5 4 3 2 1

ISBN: 978-0-7603-9565-3

Digital edition published in 2025
eISBN: 978-0-7603-9566-0

Library of Congress Control number: 2024949356

Group Publisher: Rage Kindelsperger
Creative Director: Laura Drew
Managing Editor: Cara Donaldson
Editor: Katie McGuire
Cover and Interior Design: Laura Klynstra
Cover Photograph: Dan MacMedan/Contour/Getty Images

Printed in China

This publication has not been prepared, approved, or licensed by the author, producer, or
owner of any motion picture, television program, book, game, blog, or other work referred
to herein. This is not an official or licensed publication. We recognize further that some
words, models' names, and designations mentioned herein are the property of the trademark holder. We use them for identification purposes only.